**Please return this book
on or before the last
date shown or ask for
It to be renewed.**

BEDFORD

the commercial vehicle for all purposes

2 ton sixwheeler with new styled and forward mounted engine, still retaining a long bonnet. Conversion by Carrimore

W model. 1938 styling, 30 cwt. Fitted with disc wheels, single rear tyre equipment

3 ton model with short wheelbase tipper

BEDFORD

L. Geary

IAN HENRY PUBLICATIONS

Front cover picture: 30 cwt WS model, 1932.
Special van body for Carr's Biscuits.
Normal control

© Leslie Geary, 1991

British Library Cataloguing in Publication Data

Geary, L. (Leslie)
   Bedford
   1. Bedford commercial vehicles, history
   I. Title
   629.224

   ISBN 0-86025- 437 2

Printed in Great Britain
for
Ian Henry Publications, Ltd.
20 Park Drive, Romford, Essex RM1 4LH

INTRODUCTION

Vauxhall Motors, Limited, the makers of the Bedford commercial vehicles – trucks, vans, buses and coaches – goes back to very humble beginnings when a shrewd Scottish engineer, Alexander Wilson, started his own business in 1857 under the name of the Vauxhall Ironworks to manufacture steam engines for tugs, paddle steamers and other river craft. But the name Vauxhall goes back much further than Alexander Wilson and his ironworks.

The Vauxhall crest, the griffin, came from Luton in Bedfordshire: it was the heraldic emblem of a certain nobleman, Fulk le Brèant, a soldier of fortune at the Court of King John; for his services to the King Fulk was given the Manor of Luton and a heiress, Margaret de Radvers, for a bride, both sanctioned by King John himself. Lady Margaret possessed a residence in London which her husband occupied and the house became known as Fulk's Hall. On the death of the king in 1216 the unfortunate Fulk was exiled to France where he died a poor man. His name, however, lived on, changing over the years, first to Fawke's Hall, and then to Vauxhall.

Several centuries later a famous pleasure park, Vauxhall Gardens, was laid out on the site previously occupied by the old Fulk's Hall and it was near these gardens that Alexander Wilson established his ironworks. Wilson adopted the Vauxhall griffin as his trade mark, this same griffin (a mythical creature, half eagle and half lion) which had been the crest of Fulk le Brèant on his personal standard.

By the end of the 19th century Alexander Wilson found himself in financial difficulties, so much so that a receiver had to be appointed. After a thorough investigation into Wilson's affairs, the receiver realised that there was a possibility of survival and he advised Wilson to take action and explore the possibilities of entering the new motor industry. Alexander Wilson did investigate and decided to take the receiver's advice.

In 1903 the first Vauxhall motor car made its debut. It was a popular little car with tiller steering, two seats, and a 5 horse power single cylinder petrol engine driving the rear wheels via a single chain. Fuel consumption worked out at 40 miles per gallon of fuel.

1904 and 1905 saw further developments made to the motor car by Vauxhall. The tiller steering gave way to the steering wheel and linkage. The latest models in 1905 were powered by a three cylinder petrol engine and, later still, a larger engine of four cylinders at 18 h.p. was introduced. The Vauxhall Ironworks were getting too cramped for room and larger premises were needed if Vauxhall were to advance and develop new motor car models.

In 1905 the firm obtained new premises in the small Bedfordshire town of Luton; consequently the Vauxhall Ironworks in Vauxhall Walk were vacated. With the move north went Alexander Wilson's trade mark, the Fulk le Brèant griffin and the name Vauxhall. It was rather strange that the name and the crest should return to the country seat where Fulk had resided some seven centuries earlier.

To continue with the manufacture of marine engineering products as well as the building of motor cars it was necessary to separate the two businesses. A new company, Vauxhall Motors, Limited, was formed to take care to the automobile side, leaving the Vauxhall ironworks to carry on with the marine engineering. At the start of the Great War in 1914 it was essential that Vauxhall concentrate on motor vehicles at the Luton plant and the marine engineering business gradually faded out.

During the war Vauxhall produced 2,000 staff cars for the War Office and these became a familiar sight in Flanders and many other battle grounds.

However, by the mid 20s Vauxhall's fortunes were dwindling and the company was wondering how to survive the crisis: from the other side of the Atlantic the giant American motor manufacturer, General Motors Corporation, was very eager to obtain a foothold in the United Kingdom, not by establishing a British or European company or even any dealership, but by acquiring existing facilities with a ready made manufacturing plant. They first approached the Wolseley Motor Company, known to be in financial difficulties, but Morris, anticipating the GM take-over, acquired Wolseley for themselves as a means of expansion to their own business. taken aback by Morris' move General Motors then turned their attention to Vauxhall and, after negotiations obtained in 1925 the entire ordinary share capital of Vauxhall Motor Company.

After the take-over Vauxhall still retained its name and its griffin, but had to change its policy and, instead of producing expensive high performance cars for selected customers (now a shrinking market), turn their attention to the manufacture of medium priced family saloon cars for the ever increasing motoring public on a volume basis, as a challenge to Ford, Morris and Austin.

This change over took time and the results of the General Motors/Vauxhall amalgamation and its resultant new models were not ready for the motoring public until the October of 1930. In a short time the Vauxhall car shared the popularity of the medium car market with its competitors. It was a year later, in 1931, when Vauxhall decided to enter the commercial vehicle market under the name of Bedford.

Over the years both Vauxhall cars and Bedford commercials enjoyed success, the Bedford obtaining a lead over its competitors. This competition, especially with Ford, remained like a ding-dong battle for the supreme holder of the market.

But like a lot of good things, they must come to an end. The slump in the commercial vehicle market meant Bedford lost the lead to Ford and Vauxhall experienced heavy losses, especially on the Bedford side of the business. Ford also became a victim of the slump, but survived through its merger with Fiat in the Iveco-Ford deal.

Vauxhall were not so lucky. A complete reorganisation by GM caused the medium and heavy commercial vehicle side of Vauxhall, Bedford, to cease production. The general public and operators could hardly believe the news on 9th September, 1986, that Bedford was to close and cease production. Whilst the heavy clouds still gathered over the company many people expected that Bedford would survive with help from General Motors, but it was not to be.

Agreement was reached whereby the light commercial vans and trucks, such as the CF series and the Isuzu models, were to remain in production and built in the Vauxhall car plant. The outstanding orders from the Ministry of Defence for Bedford military vehicles would continue for the time being until other arrangements could be made. The medium and heavy Bedford models simply ceased production altogether.

AWD Company, who made sixwheeler and all wheel drive conversions in the Midlands, took over the Bedford military vehicle content and purchased the good-will and the Dunstable plant with the ultimate object of reviving the medium and heavy trucks and to continue to market them as Bedford. AWD continue to produce the Bedford 4x4 TM military truck and recently there was news of the Bedford TL being back in business, the biggest change being that the Bedford diesel engine has been replaced by the Perkins 6 cylinder Phaser engine.

1931 2 ton model and 1980 38 tonne tractor unit and combination

INTO THE COMMERCIAL VEHICLE MARKET

Vauxhall did not enter the commercial vehicle market until 1931. Their first vehicle was a 2 ton payload capacity truck chassis under the banner of 'Bedford': the most obvious and likely choice of name to be adopted, which could stand the satisfactory explanation that it was taken from the county name of Bedfordshire wherein the company resided. There was, however, a saloon body which Vauxhall had named the Bedford in 1922 and it must not be confused, of course, with the London based Bedford Motor Company which, in 1912, provided bodies for the Bedford-Buick motor car.

Introduced in April, 1931, the 2 ton chassis cab version was offered with two wheelbases; short at 3.33 metres (131 inches), designated the model WHG; and the long version at 3.98 metres (157 inches), designated the model WLG. The power unit for both models was a six cylinder in-line petrol engine of 3.177 litres, overhead valves and developing 44 b.h.p. at 2400 r.p.m. The drive to the rear wheels was through a four speed crash change gearbox to a torque tube enclosed drive shaft coupled to a spiral bevel gear driven rear axle.

The new Bedford vehicle eventually replaced the Chevrolet trucks which were imported by General Motors from the U.S.A. At a glance the public thought that the new Bedford was a copy of the Chevrolet; there was a similarity, but there were many differences, mainly mechanical.

Launched into a market already dominated by much heavier vehicles, a lightweight 2 tonner was out of the ordinary. The motor trade considered that there would not be much demand for such a light vehicle, assuming that operators would prefer a more substantially built vehicle, but the trade was proved wrong. Orders demonstrated that Vauxhalls had 'got it right': success was almost immediate. Prices were such as to encourage sales and gave a boost to Vauxhall's success. The short wheelbase WHG chassis and cab version was priced at £198, the long wheelbase WLG at £210.

Following the introduction of the chassis cab versions a factory range of drop sided float bodies was announced and, when mounted on the chassis cabs formed a complete truck, still reasonably priced at £240 and £260. Next came the chassis front end versions suitable for the mounting of special bodies, especially vans for customers such as the Express Dairy and Pickfords.

Sales of the 2 ton became more widespread when, in August, 1931, Baico, the engineering company, offered chassis and wheelbase extensions and Spurling, another small engineering firm, offered six-wheeler conversions by introducing a third rearmost trailing axle. For the building and construction industry Spenborough, an engineering and body builder, built a three-way tipper body which could be mounted on the short wheelbase, WHG model.

The market demanded a lighter weight model with a lower payload and the possibility of a delivery van. Vauxhall accepted the challenge and made a great step forward in the formation of the first commercial vehicle range by introducing two additional models, a 30 cwt payload truck chassis and a 12 cwt delivery van. The 30 cwt version was designated the WS, being a lighter version of the 2 ton short wheelbase, with a lighter suspension and single rear tyre equipment, the remainder was as the 2 ton chassis. Once more, it was reasonably priced at £175 for the chassis cab version and £210 for the complete truck with drop sided float body.

The 12 cwt van, designated as model VYC, had a wheelbase of 2.69 metres (106 inches) and was powered by the 16.9 h.p., R.A.C. rating, six cylinder petrol engine, as installed in the Vauxhall 'Cadet' saloon car. The drive for the 12 cwt was through a three speed gearbox and a torque tube enclosed drive shaft to a spiral level gear driven rear axle. The price was attractive at £185, inclusive of electrical equipment and a chrome plated radiator grille surround, also available was a chassis front end version for the mounting of special bodies, priced at £135. A more powerful model version, designated VXC, similar to the VYC, but powered by the Bedford 26.3 h.p. rated six cylinder petrol engine, was available.

In November, 1931, a Bedford dealer, Atlas of Newport, arranged a novel demonstration to justify the dealer's faith in the Vauxhall commercial vehicle range. A fully laden 2 ton Bedford truck was run non-stop for seventy-two hours. Refuelling and watering were carried out when necessary whilst the vehicle was travelling at very low speed in low gear. Climbing the Monmouthshire mountain roads, unmade roads and paved highways, through all kinds of weather failed to stop the Bedford truck until it arrived home where a hero's welcome was waiting to show considerable praise for the vehicle's performance: it had covered 1,268 miles and had been limited to a maximum speed to thirty miles per hour.

During the last quarter of 1931 significant improvements were made to the 30 cwt and the 2 ton factory built vans, increasing the load capacity to 250 cubic feet with larger and wider bodies. At the beginning of 1932, less than twelve months since the first Bedford had left the Luton factory, sales were more than encouraging - 12,000 Bedford vehicles had been produced and sold.

Standard factory built cabs on 2 tonners. The second and third from the right have standard cabs: the rest of the vehicles have a variety of makes of cabs. 1931

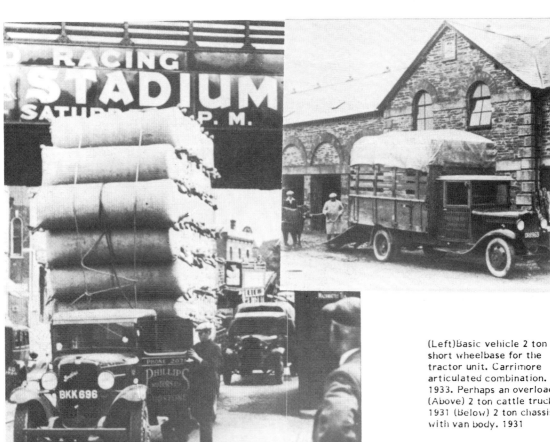

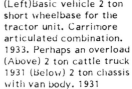

(Left)Basic vehicle 2 ton short wheelbase for the tractor unit. Carrimore articulated combination. 1933. Perhaps an overload (Above) 2 ton cattle truck 1931 (Below) 2 ton chassis with van body. 1931

Vauxhall had covered the medium range of trucks, the light machines, and larger types of vans for the market. What about the light delivery van market for local small traders such as butchers, grocers, fishmongers, plumbers and many more trades? These business people needed something much smaller than the 30 cwt or 12 cwt that Bedford could offer. Investigations showed that the market was sound for such light vehicles, with many operators pressing for a small pickup truck, as well as a van. A light 8 cwt van was introduced in 1933, based on the 12 and 14 h.p. Vauxhall six cylinder saloon car, announced the same year. The new van was designated the model ASYC, powered by the 12 h.p. six cylinder petrol engine. The drive was through a four speed gearbox, synchromesh in top and third gears only, to a spiral bevel gear driven rear axle. The model became the cheapest six cylinder petrol engine driven goods vehicle on the market. It had a generous load space of 85 cubic feet and, to make the van even more attractive, a chrome radiator grille surround was fitted, leaving the dark coloured matrix of the radiator in contrast. A pick-up version in the form of a small float truck body mounted on the chassis version of the ASYC, this was followed by a second version of the van, powered by the Vauxhall 14 h.p. six cylinder petrol engine as an optional choice and designated the model ASXC. During 1933 Bedford sales topped the 16,000 mark and, by the end of the year, the Bedford commercials were operating all over the world. Boxing of KD (knocked down) vehicles for assembly in overseas dealerships and agents became a major operation at the Luton plant.

To offer something different for the 12 cwt van for the 1933 market a small face lift was made by fitting wire spoke wheels and a synchromesh gearbox. The Commercial Motor Show that November opened with something of a sensation on

2 ton short wheelbase
modified to take a
semi-trailer with
furniture removal
body, 1933

Sixwheeler with
pantechnicon body.
Conversion by fitting
third axle. Dual rear
tyre equipment, 1932

the Vauxhall/Bedford stand. The new Bedford 3 ton payload chassis cab, the model
WT, featuring a short bonnet, almost towards a semi-forward control, was
launched. The layout had been achieved by moving the engine forward, locating
the centre line of the engine directly over the front axle. The WT was powered by
the well tried 3.177 litre petrol engine used on the 2 ton, but the engine's power
had been increased to 60 b.h.p, mainly due to improved carburation using a down-
draft designed carburettor. Two wheelbases were available; short at 2.83 metres
(110 inches), designated the model WTH, 508 mm (20 inches) shorter than the 2 ton,
although the same long wheelbase as the 2 ton was retained, the model WTL, at
3.98 metres (157 inches).

The model series was remarkable in another way – it remained under the magic
figure of 50 cwt (2054 kgs) unladen weight, permitting the vehicle to travel at 30
m.p.h. maximum speed, also in a reduced taxation class. Vehicles about the 50 cwt
unladen weight were only permitted to travel at 20 m.p.h. maximum, with a higher
taxation bracket.

An advertisement appeared in the press on the new Bedford 3 ton truck as 'The
truck for 50% overload'. Whilst it really meant to draw the attention to the toughness of the model in those days of less stringent regulations, this overload was
widely used and even exceeded by many operators, especially in the tipper field,
where the short wheelbase model WTH at 2.83 metres fitted with a tipper body was
affected. This chassis cab version became very popular among small and even
larger construction companies.

Model WS, 30 cwt truck 1932. This was in daily use by A Powrie of Abernyte, near Dundee, until 1977

1934, WS, 30 cwt van and model VYC 12 cwt van with wire wheels for Carr's Biscuits. Normal control 12 h.p., 8 cwt van, model ASYC on its rounds. Fitted with wire wheels.

Publicity for the new 3 ton model WT. Advertising the whole Bedford range: 8 cwt, 12 cwt, 30 cwt, 2 ton and the new 3 ton. November, 1933

1934 deserves a mention, apart from any design changes to Vauxhall's products: that July the Bedford Drivers' Club was formed, an innovation to be copied by other vehicle manufacturers. This exclusive club offered free insurance to the drivers and built up a recommended chain of eating places and rest homes, as well as offering some means of relaxation. The Club continued to support and help drivers with their problems, including any court case they might get involved in, until economic pressure led to its disbandment in 1968. 1934 also saw changes to the design of the drive lines for the 30 cwt and 2 ton models, the introduction of the Hotchkiss drive system, the open drive shaft, the replacement of the torque tube enclosed drive shaft and incorporated a tipped rear axle housing to improve the drive alignment with the rear axle spiral bevel drive pinion.

Later, in 1935, a face lift was given to the 30 cwt, the model WS and the 2 ton, models WHG and WLG, bringing them more into line with the 3 tonner, the model with the 'bulldog' look. However, whilst these models did not receive the full styling treatment, still retaining their long bonnets, they matched the forward mounted 3 ton in general looks and did include the forward mounted engine, the cabs having been moved forward, reducing the distance between the rear of the cab and the centre line of the front axle, thus assisting in reducing the wheelbase, while still retaining the same float body length. The 30 cwt, model WS, and the short wheelbase 2 ton, model WHG, were reduced to 3.048 metres (120 inches) and

8 cwt pick-up, wooden float body, 1933

3 ton truck carrying hay in the Yorkshire Dales

First 3 ton delivered to operator. Sussex sandpit

1935 revised and restyled 30 cwt with forward mounted engine and new radiator grille

11

the 2 ton long wheelbase, the model WLG, reduced to 3.63 metres (143 inches).

1935 also brought changes to the 8 cwt models ASYC and ASXC, by fitting a vacuum advance device to the distributor, offering full width driver's seat and a hand operated starter switch on the instrument panel to replace the foot operated switch on the cab floor. Finally, a vertical grille was fitted and the headlamp tie bar was removed on the 12 cwt models VXC and VYC. By the end of 1935 the 12 cwt models VXC and VYC were replaced by the 20 h.p. powered BYC and the 26 h.p. powered BXC. The changes reflected the arrival of the Vauxhall Big Six saloon cars for 1935/36. However, no changes were made to the 8 cwt 'A' vans, which continued in production with the 12 h.p. and the 14 h.p. petrol engines.

The strengthen and reduce cost of the steering connecting rod, the drag link, on the 30 cwt and 2 ton models a new design of rod was introduced. Made from a forging of 'H' section with integral ball joints ends, this replaced the old design made from a tubular rod with screwed on ball joints.

Production of the Bedford vehicles proceeded with success and, by the end of 1937, the truck range topped 26,000 vehicles per annum, with the 3 ton proving very popular. Small changes were made to the range during 1937, like a Zenith 30 VIG carburettor and a new exhaust manifold thermostat valve for the 8 cwt models, ASYC and ASXC; a thermostat was added to the cooling system of the petrol engine for the 12 cwt, BYC and BXC, 30 cwt WS and the 2 ton WHG and WLG, and the 3 ton WHT and WLT.

To the end of March, 1938, the smallest commercial vehicle in the Bedford range was the 8 cwt 'A' series, powered by the 12 and 14 h.p. petrol engine. The arrival of a yet lighter van brought the smallest end of the range down to 5/6 cwt. It had been the introduction of the light Vauxhall car, the 10 h.p. model 'K', which gave Vauxhall the opportunity to create a 5/6 cwt van for the Bedford commercial

5/6 cwt model H series. HC model 5/6 cwt van, 1938

range. Designated as the model HC, it offered a load space of 70 cubic feet and claimed a fuel consumption of 35 miles per gallon. This model remained in production until mid 1948.

In the summer of 1938 important changes were made to the 'W' series, 30 cwt, 2 and 3 ton versions. These included the installation of a new 28 h.p. petrol engine with increased power from 64 to 72 b.h.p., a new radiator grille and a general tidy up of the front end appearance and the radiator filler cap was relocated under the bonnet. One new additional model version was released, a factory built tipper body on the 3 ton, model WHT, the short wheelbase of 2.79 metres (110 inches) at a very interesting price of £330.

The fateful year of 1939 had Bedford bringing new offerings to the transport industry. A new range of Bedford vehicles was being prepared to replace the existing 'W' series, which had first appeared in 1931. This new range appeared in the spring of 1939 with the first purpose built models, K, M and O. Although announced before the start of World War II, real production was not to be accomplished until after the war in 1945. There were other design changes to the Bedford range with the introduction of the 6 cwt Utility Wagon with a small wooden float body, mounted on the chassis cab version of the model HC on 1st January, 1939. In June, 1939, a larger version of the HC van, a 10/12 cwt capacity van, the model JC, with a wheelbase of 2.667 metres (105 inches), powered by the 12 h.p. Vauxhall petrol engine was announced. The introduction of the larger van saw the demise of the 8 cwt ASYC and ASXC models and the 12 cwt BYC and BXC models.

There was nothing new in seeing a Bedford articulated combination. From 1931 specialist conversions had been offered, notably by Carrimore and, later, by Scammell Lorries of Watford. These conversions were merely standard short wheelbase truck chassis cabs modified to accommodate a fifth wheel coupling to accept the coupling of a semi-trailer. Bedford marketed an articulated tractor unit which was the result of a joint venture between Bedford and Scammell. The rear of the Bedford 3 ton short wheelbase chassis had been modified to enable the fitting of the automatic trailer coupling as used on the Scammell three wheeled 3 and 6 ton mechanical horse models. The coupling enabled the Bedford tractor to couple and uncouple automatically from the semi-trailer without the driver leaving his cab.

The war clouds thickened and grew darker and eventually war broke out. Time had now come for Vauxhall to turn its attention to the design of Bedford models for military use, to supply the fighting forces and to don its khaki dress.

6 cwt
model HC pick-up,
1938

13

THE CALL TO ARMS

On 3 September, 1939, 'Call to Arms' was the Government's request to the British motor industry. With civilian production at a standstill Bedford answered the call with a range of military transport trucks. The 15 cwt infantry truck model 'MW'. 30 cwt general service truck models 'OX and 'OY' and the one to become famous, the model 'QL' four wheel drive 3 ton general service truck.

During the Second World War Vauxhall more than answered the call to arms, as through the years of conflict Bedfords made a special mark with the British Tommies and Allied Forces. More than 250,000 Bedford trucks went into service, filling most military roles. A high proportion of this production was the 15 cwt MW, with its various roles; the model MWC, a water tanker; the MWR, fitted for wireless; the MWT, anti-tank gun tractor; the MVW, general service van; and there were others to meet special requirements by the War Office.

The War Office had issued tenders as far back as 1935 for vehicles suitable for His Majesty's Forces for a 15 cwt infantry truck. In 1937 Vauxhall produced the W.D. prototype and submitted it for testing, which was carried out in North Wales. The vehicle submitted proved successful and the first fifty 15 cwt MW commenced production in August, 1939, to be used as towing vehicles for the 2 pounder anti-tank gun and carriage. Early models of the MW had open cabs, small separate folding windscreens, metal half doors and detachable perspex side screens. Powered by Bedford 3.5 litre six cylinder petrol engine developing 72 b.h.p, the drive line was through a four speed gearbox to a spiral bevel gear driven rear axle. Its wheelbase was 2.525 metres (99 inches).

The 30 cwt models OX and OY, based on the latest civilian production normal control, provided transport for the troops and general service operations. The QL

1939/45 Fleet of tractor units and articulated combinations. 'Queen Mary' aircraft semi-trailers

Army Fire Service. Model QL 4x4 military truck with full tilt over float body

15 cwt MW model infantry truck. Note: no doors, individual windscreens and canvas canopy hood, 1939

four wheel drive, 3 ton forward control performed many tasks on the Second Front and the Middle East theatres of war.

In addition to truck production Vauxhall were asked to further their war effort in the production of Churchill tanks. Their answer was the production of 5,640 tanks, some of which came from the 'shadow' factories, having been built from assemblies and components manufacturers at the Luton factory.

A different request came later from the Ministry to Vauxhall, not more vehicles nor more tanks, but the supply of a tank engine. The first 120 b.h.p tank engine built at Luton was a remarkable achievement, designed on the drawing board, built, developed and tested for production in only 89 days.

Bedford, like Ford, Morris, Austin and Commer, contributed to the enormous task of supplying vehicles for all purposes to aid the British and Allied Forces throughout the war to ultimate victory.

3 ton 4x4 QL model truck in Victory Celebration Parade through the streets of Luton, 1945
1945, 5 ton long wheelbase on dockside

FORTY YEARS OF PEACE

Towards the end of 1945 the Luton factory began to prepare for civilian production once more, after six years of supplying vehicles for the mighty world conflict. The new civilian range which had been announced in the early part of 1939 was re-introduced. There was no money or enough raw materials to arrange any new design of models. The pre-war designed vehicles still had the normal control classification: the K rated at the new dual loading 30/40 cwt, replacing the 30 cwt model WS; the M rated at the new dual loading of 2/3 ton, replacing the 2 ton models WHG and WLG; the earlier 3 ton models WHT and WLT became OS, short wheelbase, and OL, long wheelbase, rated at a dual loading of 3/4 tons.

For the first time Bedford entered the medium heavy market in the 5 ton bracket. With the 5 ton models, OSB, short wheelbase, and OLB, long wheelbase, was the model OSS, a tractor unit. The new models, K, M and O, were little changed mechanically from the old W equivalents. Load ratings were higher and they had a new feature in hydraulic brakes. However, the new 5 ton's unladen weight of just under 50 cwt qualified for the 30 m.p.h. legal maximum speed limit and reduced taxation. The main difference was visually, with the new monoshell driver's cab and in it a two piece shallow 'V' formation windscreen, well designed and bringing a new style and levels of comfort.

Vauxhall offered the market a complete range of commercials from 5 cwt to 5 tons in payload ratings and a 8 ton Bedford-Scammell tractor unit.

The introduction of the new range advanced Bedford's already strong hold of the domestic market. Vast improvements in penetration of the markets increased export sales. With the success already achieved the range remained in production from 1945 to 1953.

In October, 1946, Vauxhall celebrated the ten thousandth Bedford to be exported since the end of the war, that particular vehicle left the Bedford plant for Istanbul: the majority of exported vehicles at this time were the new 5 ton model O.

Later in 1946 the power unit installed in the 5/6 cwt model was replaced by the 12 h.p. petrol engine already in use in the model JC, 10/12 cwt model; one step towards commonising engines for the van ranges. The little 5/6 cwt van continued in production until the end of September, 1948.

Another important milestone was reached when, on 22nd October, 1947, the Minister of Supply, George Strauss, drove the millionth Bedford produced in Luton .off the assembly line and the Vauxhall employee who had driven the first Bedford off the line in 1931 accompanied the Minister.

The later forties were quiet years, with no visually exciting new models, just the K, M and O series, chassis and trucks, continuing to keep success at home and overseas. However, the autumn of 1948 did see some activity with the last of the small 5/6 cwt off the assembly line and the JC 10/12 cwt redesignated as the model PC, fitted with a three speed gearbox and having steering column gear change. From 1948 the PC was Bedford's only offering in the van sector remaining in production, until the innovation in vans, the model CA, was announced in 1952.

Model OL, 5 ton long wheelbase, 157 inches. In New Zealand
Model ML, 2/3 ton long wheelbase. Operating for the National Coal Board in late 1940s

Forward control conversion. Vans on K series 30 cwt chassis, and (below) 5 ton OLB forward control conversion with tilt cab by Nevills

5 ton with Nevills tilt cab and forward control conversion refuse collection body. Cab fully tilted and resting on the struts

The dual rating of the K, 30/40 cwt, replacing the early WS 30 cwt did not last long, as by October, 1948, the K was back in the single load rating of 30 cwt. The late summer of 1948 saw the K van being offered with a sliding side loading door as a space saving feature, leaving the actual cab doors still of the hinged slam-type design. Forward control versions of the K, M and O models were offered by Nevilles, the body builder, which also included the feature of a tilt cab.

Vauxhall were always improving power to weight ratio on their Bedford chassis for better vehicle performance. In 1950 a new petrol engine range was provided, designated the 'Extra Duty' engine, a six cylinder in-line developing 84 b.h.p. for the 3/4 ton and the 5 ton and a 75 b.h.p. version for the 30 cwt and the 2/3 ton models.

The Luton plant required some relief with a turnover of almost 39,000 commercials produced in 1949, together with a car production of 45,000 – the factory was getting somewhat overcrowded. The matter became urgent, so a £10M expansion plan was launched, spread over four years, commencing with a new site of some 19½ acres on which a new production plant was built.

On the Vauxhall/Bedford stand at the 1950 London Commercial Motor Show was exhibited a new 7 ton range, the 'S' model, a forward control range. This was Bedford's attempt to enter the heavier vehicle market. Whilst forward control conversions had previously been carried out on Bedford trucks and the QL four wheel drive forward control had been introduced during the war, this was Bedford's first attempt to produce a civilian forward control range. The S models series was introduced with four wheelbases and with factory built bodies for tippers and trucks. The wheelbases were 2.946 metres (116 inches) for the short version; a 3.96 metres (156 inches) long version; a shorter wheelbase of 2.18 metres (86 inches) for the Bedford-Scammell 10 ton articulated tractor unit; and, finally, an extra long wheelbase of 5.23 metres (206 inches) for a bus or coach chassis. For power a new 300 cubic inch, six cylinder in-line petrol engine developing 110 b.h.p. was introduced. Drive line was through a new four speed synchromesh gearbox to a hypoid bevel gear driven rear axle. The hypoid bevel gear driven rear axle was something new for Bedford and gave improved gear tooth strength for the extra heavy duty operation expected. This new S range went into production in the new 19½ acre extension plant at Luton and remained in production, with continuing success, until late in 1960, when it was replaced by the model TK range, forward control.

The smaller Bedfords underwent changes to update them to market requirements. The K, M and O models were given new payload ratings: the 2/3 ton model became 3 tons; the 3/4 ton model became 4 tons; whilst the 5 ton remained as it was. This was not the end of the uprating; gearboxes with synchromesh top, third and second gear replaced the existing gearboxes and the 4 and 5 tonners now received the new hypoid bevel gear driven rear axle.

1950 was not a good time to introduce anything new, such as the much-needed 7 ton range. Although orders were high production had to be cut back, simply because of the national shortage of sheet steel, which had to become rationed.

The first production of the CA van, 10/12 cwt model, had one wheelbase only at 2.28 metres (90 inches) with a cubic capacity of load space of 135 cubic feet. It was a semi-forward control, with sliding doors each side, an all steel body and quite a lively performance, powered by the 1507 cc 'square' petrol engine used in the Vauxhall 'E' type 'Wyvern' saloon car. The price was as encouraging as had been

10 ton articulated
combination. Single
axle semi-trailer
with tanker body &
short wheelbase
S series tractor unit

7 ton truck long
wheelbase, 157
inches. S series
forward control
with standard
float type
body, 1950

Military 4x4 R type with
S series cab. Undergoing
rough country trials

First production in March, 1952, of the Bedford van. Model CA, 10 cwt, Mark 11. Semi-forward control

all the Bedford commercials at £400, with purchase tax adding a further £81. The CA success was almost immediate and the number of orders received were such that, between its inauguration in 1952 and when it ceased production in 1969, over 370,000 had been built, not only for domestic consumption, but also for the overseas market. Body styles mounted on the chassis cab version and conversions of the van body included ambulances, buses, ice-cream vans, mobile shops, tower wagons, livestock carriers, mini-pantechnicons and light tippers.

In the usual Ministry of Defence role of increasing and improving the armed forces' transport they issued tenders within the motor industry for various types of vehicles. Bedford was one of the manufacturers submitting a military 4 x 4 based on the model 'S' forward control chassis. It was designated as the 'R' series 3 ton general purpose vehicle and, having successfully undergone inspection and testing, was adopted by the British military authorities, later to see service in many overseas countries. It continued in production until 1970, ten years after the 'S' series had terminated.

After fifteen years of service and the production of some 412,000, the models K, M and O light medium weight normal control range ceased and were replaced by the 'A' series. Inheriting most of its predecessors mechanical features, the 'A' series featured an entirely new cab, which was a complete breakaway from the narrow front end of the earlier models. The wide front normal control featured a 3 slatted grille and headlamps incorporated in the front wings with decorative wing flashings accommodating the side lamps. There were four basic chassis with wheelbases ranging from 3.022 metres (119 inches) to 4.242 metres (167 inches), including the 4 ton short wheelbase chassis cab for the basis of the 8 ton articulated tractor unit. They were powered by the heavy duty petrol engine range; 76 b.h.p. version for the 20/25 cwt and 3 ton models and the 84 b.h.p. for the heavier chassis of 4 tons plus.

Bedford joined competition by offering a fully factory installed diesel engine as an optional power unit. The diesel engine chosen was the Perkins P6, six cylinder in-line engine made available in the 4 and 5 ton models and the 8 ton tractor unit. To complete the introduction of diesel power the heavier 'S' range (7 tons) was offered with the Perkins R6, six cylinder in-line diesel developing 108 b.h.p in 1953, as an optional power unit to the Bedford uprated 300 cubic inch petrol unit, which was increased in power to 115 b.h.p.

By 1954 Vauxhall's Bedford commercials had reached 58,292 production, which was more than satisfactory, so much so that more space was needed to both maintain and improve the output. Negotiations for a new factory at Dunstable were completed and production proceeded with the first Bedford rolling off the assembly line on 2 August, 1955.

By mid-1956 the option of a diesel four cylinder in-line engine developing 55 b.h.p. was available for the 25/35 cwt chassis (uprated in load capacity from the 20/25 cwt version) and the 2/3 ton chassis. During the same year minor changes were made, the 25/30 cwt replacing the 25/35 cwt chassis, the 2/3 ton became the 2 ton, and a new long wheelbase 3 ton was introduced; all four still offered the option of the Perkins P4 diesel engine.

The market demanded constant improvements to the models and, to meet the demand, Vauxhall decided to have a complete review of their Bedford commercial range, then to consider any necessary changes. Additional model versions, new model designations, including revised ratings, and even face-lifts were made. Up to fifty models were offered to the market, rather a complicated set-up to

A series, normal control. Note its predecessor on the right

describe with justice. However, the following will present a brief summary of the model line-up.

§ The normal control lightweight and middle weight chassis were redesignated the 'D' series, although visually similar to the 'A' series, improvements were made. Models were 25 and 35 cwt chassis; 2 ton and 3 ton chassis lightweights; 4, 5 and 6 ton middle weights, including the 8 ton tractor unit. All normal control.

§ A new forward control set of models designated the 'C' series': 4, 5 and 6 ton chassis, with a slightly revised version of the 'S' type cab.

§ The 6 ton models, both normal and forward control ranges, 'D' and 'C' were entirely new vehicles offered in four wheelbases from 3.048 metres (120 inches) to 4.242 metres (167 inches), which filled the gap between the 5 and 7 ton models.

The latest 'S' type cab was also used on the 'C' models to rationalise and was distinguishable by the new chrome surround to the radiator grille with the name 'Bedford' now on top of the radiator grille. Further rationalisation was with the middle weights normal control 'D' series, 4 tons upwards, taking the same cab as their smaller companions, but distinguished by a slightly wider grille slat design and with a chrome strip for the upper slat. The broad specification of the CA van range remained unchanged as did the specification for the R range 4 x 4.

Vauxhall had been working for some time on diesel engines entailing quite a deal of development. However, Bedford was rewarded in 1957 by the announcement of their own designed and built diesel engine, which was a 300 cubic inch capacity, six cylinder, vertical four stroke in-line, developing 97 b.h.p at 2300 r.p.m.: the torque capacity was good at 800 r.p.m. and with the maximum torque at low revs. enabled the vehicle to steadily climb good gradients and pull out of poor ground, which was advantageous for tipper operation. The engine had a long life and was the set pattern for further Bedford diesels. However, development in the engine range as a whole had not been idle; the old faithful 'Extra Duty' petrol version was revised to become the 214 cu.in. power unit, developing 100 b.h.p (16 more than

A series. 4 ton short wheelbase, normal control tractor unit with semi-trailer, 1953

(Left) A series, normal control with styled van body (Right) A series, normal control tipper, 1956

before). The 300 cu.in. petrol engine, introduced in 1950 for the S range was also improved including a new cylinder block. Vauxhall could now offer a good range of engines for the Bedford commercials; five power choice, the new 300 cu.in diesel; the 214 cu.in. petrol engine and still retained the Perkins P4 192 cu.in and, for the 300 cu.in. petrol, the heavier range of vehicle the Perkins R6 340 cu.in.

The achievements for 1957 were not yet complete – there was more to come! The 'D' types were a short term series and were to be replaced with a new permanent truck range and, even at the time the D was introduced, their

D series. Heavy model, types 4, 5, and 6 tons
Vehicle leaving Meccano factory, Liverpool. 1957

New look cab for S series. This vehicle had been modified for a Swiss steel merchant to a one man cab to carry long lengths of steel bars and tubes, 1957

replacements were well on the way on both drawing board and with the development engineers; it was only a matter of time. Then, in the closing months of 1957, came a second Bedford designed and built diesel engine, a smaller capacity 200 cu.in, producing 64 b.h.p. at 2000 r.p.m., suitable for the 25 cwt and the 3 ton chassis. For drive lines, Bedford announced their own two speed rear axle for use on vehicles of 4 ton capacity and over. The CA van wheel and tyre equipment was replaced by 15 inch wheels and tyres to give a lower loading height.

On 28 May, 1958, Vauxhall hit the jackpot again, but this time it was an even

greater jackpot, the one millionth Bedford vehicle, an 'S' type model 7 tonner, powered by the Bedford diesel engine went down the assembly line; however further gains were made when it was revealed that 360,000 of this first million had been exported.

More news for 1958, this time at the Commercial Motor Show, was a complete new Bedford normal control range of vehicles designated as the model TJ range. Payload capacities were from 25 cwt to 7 tons, with an 8 ton tractor unit. Eleven models spanned wheelbases from 3.022 metres (119 inches) to 4.546 metres (179 inches). The new models had the same broad mechanical specification as their predecessors, the 'D' model series. The newly styled cab and front end separated the lighter models from the heavier with a different style of radiator grille and front panel; vertical grille slats and headlamp eyebrows for the lighter models up to 4 tons payload and horizontal grille slats for the heavier payloads. Included in the range was a low loader 4 ton payload model equipped with 16 inch wheels and tyres, a 7 ton tipper, and a 4.876 metre (16 feet) long drop sided float body for delivery work, all in addition to the standard models. Tight turning circles for manoeuvrability and low platform heights made the TJ range attractive and popular, the drivers liking the low step and the roomy three seater cab. This vehicle range, with many more improvements made over the years, lasted for over twenty years. In 1978 and 1979 the TJ was still the big seller in a number of markets, notably in Asia and Africa, although the range was no longer available for the European customer.

In 1959 what more improvements could Vauxhall make to the Bedford range, already a popular name in the transport world? Two changes were made to the CA van range; first a one piece curved windscreen and revised grille were introduced, then another wheelbase – longer at 2.59 metres (102 inches) – was added to the range to provide more available load space.

12 seater Spurling
crew cab mounted
on 25 cwt D series
and (below) Two
styles of front end
for TJ series normal
control trucks.
Horizontal slats in
the grille for the
heavier models over
4 tons; vertical
grille slats and
eyebrow headlamps
for the models
up to 4 tons

TJ model normal
control tipper.
3 ton on 119 inch
wheelbase

30

The '50s ended with the introduction of the Leyland 351 cu.in. diesel engine in the new version of the 'S' type articulated tractor unit of 12 tons capacity. The decision to instal the Leyland engine was probably taken as an interim measure until a larger capacity Bedford diesel, which was on the drawing board, was finally developed. Also at the end of the 1950s a longer wheelbase of 4.267 metres (168 inches) for the 7 ton 'S' series model was introduced to meet the demand for a 5.486 metre (18 feet) truck float body.

In less than twenty years the Bedford range of commercials had been improved and enlarged and proved to be highly successful, certainly unrecognisable from the first truck chassis which left the Luton plant assembly line in 1931.

***

1960 started a new era in the life of the Bedfords, beginning with probably the biggest advance ever made in vehicle design and cab styling, hailed as a pace setter in truck design from the outset. They called it the model 'TK' series, creating a new concept and new standards in driver environment and profitable load carrying. The 'TK' was a new location of cab ahead of engine, where the driver and passengers sat in front of the engine, instead of alongside it. With the cab step located ahead of the front axle a short front axle to the rear of the cab dimension was achieved, providing a longer body load space and better axle load distribution. Could this design have been influenced by General Motors, who were already developing trucks on similar lines in the States? Classified as a forward control, the flat floor of the cab, combined with the low step height, meant that the driver could reach his seat from either door with new found ease, as could the two passengers. Quiet, comfortable, marvellous vision, and cool – these were the working conditions for the driver which, it was claimed, reduced fatigue, thus increasing driver efficiency.

The Bedford TK had more to offer than Ford or Commer with their equivalent forward control vehicles. However, there was one feature missing, one which

Lancashire operator's fleet of 35 cwt TJ normal control chassis cab with box van body

31

The highly successful 10/12 cwt CA. Originally released with one short wheelbase, later to be offered with a longer wheelbase

operators were expecting – a tilt cab. This was rather odd, as the tilt cab was already being developed in America by both G.M.C. and Ford. There were two thoughts regarding the necessity for a tilt cab, some for and some against, but finally, the Vauxhall team considered that there was enough access via the removal of hinged lift panels supplied to enable adequate everyday servicing to be carried out without the need for a tilt cab. This was made more surprising as Ford was busy with the design of their 'D' series truck range, incorporating a tilt cab, at about the same time as the TK was being launched.

Outstanding low loading heights were created by fitting small diameter wheel and tyre equipment; 16 inch diameter for up to 5 tons payload capacity and 17 inch diameter for the 5 and 6 tons payload capacity models. The low loading height had a special appeal to users in the retail distribution trade involving unloading goods manually from the truck body platform to ground level on multi-drop delivery journeys.

Initially twelve model versions, between 3 and 6 tons payload, were released, including a 12 ton articulated tractor unit. Petrol and diesel engines, four and five speed gearboxes provided the power drive line. From the start the design on the minimum weight TK concept allowed for chassis lengthening and shortening by specialists to suit special operating requirements. These conversions were durability assured by extensive fatigue testing.

Of the earlier heavier 'S' range two versions remained in production, the 'R' model 4 x 4, which retained the 'S' cab for some years, and the long wheelbase, the 'SB' bus/coach chassis.

The 'JO' model, a normal control ½ ton pick-up, was an unorthodox creature announced to fill the request for pick-up models. A light chassis was designed on which was mounted the 'TJ' normal control cab and front end. The 'JO' was powered by the Vauxhall car engine, a 2.651 litre six cylinder petrol. Unfortunately, this pick-up was not a resounding success and did not reign long.

Once more the Ministry of Defence issued tenders for vehicles to the motor industry, amongst them being requirements for four wheel drive machines. This

Model TK, forward control. Model shown is a 5 ton with 16 inch wheels and a pantechnicon body

Model JO ½ ton normal control pick-up. Using TJ cab and the Vauxhall 2.6 litre petrol engine

time, 1962, a 4 x 4 version of the 'TJ' normal control was submitted to meet the request and was accepted, designated as the 'T5S' model.

Whilst the 'TK' series took the headlines, improvements were being made on other models. In mid-1961 the CA van models were given an optional diesel engine with the installation of the Perkins Four99 four cylinder in-line unit.

At the 1962 Show more 'TK' models were launched with displays of an 8 ton rigid 4 x 2, a 7 cubic yard tipper, and a heavy tractor unit. At that time York Trailer Company introduced a sixwheeler conversion for the 'TK' approved by Vauxhall. In October, 1962, Bedford heralded the building of the 50,000th 'TK' and, to follow this memorable year, the Sales Department boasted that they cold supply a Bedford to suit any purpose. So varied had the specifications become that it was possible that not one vehicle of any model version of the 50,000 had exactly the same specification. Variations included wheelbases, engine, gearboxes, rear axles, wheel and tyre equipment, sixwheeler conversions, wheelbase extensions and shortened wheelbases, as well as the availability of R O Ps (Regular Production Options). For the lack of a Bedford designed diesel engine with sufficient power these latest models in the heavier range in the early 1960s were powered by the Leyland 400 cu.in. six cylinder in-line diesel engine.

One of the biggest single categories of operators since the early days of the TK series had been the brewing and soft drinks industry - like Coca Cola in Hong Kong, Guinness in Ireland and Bass Charrington in England. To cater for such special needs Vauxhall set up a Bedford Special Vehicle Order Department, an extension of the Bedford engineering facilities. In the U.K. industry in general took advantage of the Bedford S.V.O. system for many specialist vehicles.

In the following two years there were improvements to the CA vans and the introduction of a new 10/12 ton heavy payload chassis - a conversion of the 7 ton TK model to a sixwheeler by Boughton and marketed as the Bedford-Boughton rigid six wheeler.

Standard 5 cubic yard tipper on 131 inch wheelbase, civilian version of the R series 4x4
Bedford/Boughton sixwheeler conversion on 7 ton model TK series. Front end tipper with twin rams, 1963

The Bedford van collection. The HA, announced in 1964, alongside CA van and a 35 cwt TJ van

The small vans with which Bedford had earlier satisfied the market of small traders had been derivatives of Vauxhall saloon cars. Such a model was the 'AS' 8 cwt van, first produced in 1933, a derivative of the 12 and 14 h.p. saloon car. Then came the AS replacement, the HC model, 5 cwt introduced in 1938, from Vauxhall's 'H' type saloon car which ceased production in 1948, with no replacement for many years. It was not until the summer of 1960 when Bedford returned to the small van market by announcing the 'HA' models, 5 and 8 cwt based on the Vauxhall 'Viva' saloon. The van models had a good load space capacity of 2.5 cubic metres (88 cu.ft.) with car comfort for the driver and with low initial cost. They were designated HA110 and HA130 models, becoming Bedford's long-lived and thoroughly proven vans and the repeated choice of many operators. The two vans remained in production until the 1980s. The HA110 had a gross vehicle weight of 1120 kgs (2480 lb) and a maximum load capacity of 356 kgs (784 lb), including driver, passenger and any equipment. With a wheelbase of 2.32 metres (91.3 inches) and powered by 1,256 litre four cylinder in-line petrol engine developing 42.5 b.h.p, it had a drive line through a four speed all synchromesh gearbox to a hypoid bevel gear driven rear axle. The HA130 was similar, but equipped with a heavy duty rear axle and heavier suspension to cater for a gross vehicle weight of 1320 kgs (2910 lb) and a maximum payload capacity of 531 kgs (1170 lb), including driver, passenger and any equipment.

Having obtained a successful market with the TK, more model versions were added to the range in 1965 – such additions as payload capacities of 30 cwt and 2 tons and a short wheelbase of 3.048 metres (120 inches) for a tipper grossing at 11682.5 kgs (11.5 tons or 25760 lb).

Vauxhall were ever seeking wider fields of operation for their Bedford trucks. When the Construction and Use Regulations were changed and re-issued by the Ministry of Transport, advising the motor industry that the maximum gross vehicle

TK articulated combination. Joint effort between Bedford and Tasker Trailer Company. Conversion of Bedford TK 4 and 5 ton chassis to 84 inch wheelbase to accommodate Tasker's automatic trailer

TK series models were extended to the lightweight versions in 1965. Payloads of 30 cwt, 2 and 3 tons.

Vehicle shown is 2 ton model

(Below) Fleet of Bedford KM series models, 14 to 22 tons gross weights, 1966

M model 4x4 with TK cab and mechanicals. Twin ram underfloor tipper bodies

weight on two axles had been increased to 16 tons, Bedford responded by announcing the KM heavy range of vehicles, covering 14 to 22 tons gross weight. In fact, the KM was an upward extension of the TK series, with a slightly heavier frame assembly and heavier suspension, etc., still maintaining the TK cab. The distinguishable outside appearance was the fitting of hefty double front bumpers. An extra long wheelbase of 5.60 metres (224 inches) was introduced to accommodate the demand for a 6.7 metre (22 feet) long float body, designated as the model KMH, which was the longest wheelbase on any Bedford.

In the development of the KM heavy duty models a new Bedford diesel engine was created, a 466 cu.in. six cylinder in-line developing 145 b.h.p and, later, a small version of 388 cu.in capacity. With this new power unit there was now sufficient power within the family of engines to suit all the Bedford range.

Two new models were announced in the summer of 1968: a TK tractor unit for articulated combination suitable for local delivery work, followed by four factory built rigid sixwheeler versions within the KM range of up to 22349 kgs (22 tons or 49286 lb) gross weight.

One and a half million Bedford trucks and chassis had been built by 24th March, 1969. The honour went to a KM 16 ton gross weight model driven off the end of the assembly line by the Minister of Technology, Anthony Wedgwood Benn, and went overseas, meaning that 49% of the 1½ million had been exported. However, in the previous year as much as 62% of production had travelled to 118 overseas countries.

The 60s closed in Bedford bidding farewell to the CA van and light truck series and hailing the appearance of its successor, the CF series. After 17 years and a production of 31,044 machines, the CA retired. The new CF series was introduced with five basic models, the 14, 18, 22, 25 and 35 cwt payloads with wheelbases of 2.69 metres (106 inches) and 3.2 metres (126 inches), featuring sliding doors and hinged doors for driver, passenger and cargo. It was powered by a choice of two petrol engines and two diesels with a drive line through a four speed synchromesh

Another model TK conversion. The cheapest method to increase the payload. Twin steer, addition of a second front axle. 14½ tons gross weight

gearbox to a hypoid bevel gear driven rear axle. There was single rear tyre equipment for the 14 to 25 cwt models and dual rear tyre equipment for the 35 cwt model. The 1960s had watched the Bedford commercial vehicle range grow, improve and hold the market with enthusiasm. What did the 1970s bring?

* * *

The 70s continued with the expansion of Bedford's drive into the market with almost any type of transport vehicle imaginable. The R model four wheel drive chassis was due for retirement. Having replaced the S series by the TK, it was only common sense that the one single model left of the S type, the R 4 x 4, should be replaced by a four wheel drive version of the TK range for economical production. A new four wheel drive series duly appeared with a new designation, the model 'M', for both military and civilian operation. A prototype TK 4 x 4 in line with the latest W.D. specifications and requirements was submitted to the Ministry of Defence for inspection and test and was accepted to replace the model 'R'. It was not long before the 'M' models became as popular with the forces as the previous machines.

In 1971, after forty years of Bedford production, more improvements were announced, such as automatic transmission option for the CF van and light truck range; three double drive sixwheelers (6 x 4) introduced for the KM range at 20/22 tons gross vehicle weights; a larger engine of 1256 cc four cylinder petrol for the HA vans; and, for economy operation which was to take preference over power performance, a special economy four cylinder petrol engine developing 24.1 b.h.p was announced for the HA110 model version as an optional power unit. The Post Office placed its first order of 2,000 for HA series vans with more large orders to follow.

Model KM sixwheeler double drive. 20/22 tons GVW. Single front end telescopic ram operated tipper

Show time again, 1972, Earl's Court, London: the Vauxhall/Bedford stand exhibited its usual share of new models. One was a tractor unit for 32 gross combination weight, based on the KM with the General Motors Detroit Diesel 6V-71 installed. Other exhibits were the new improved 'TK/M' driver's cab; a new 16 ton; a 3.759 metres (148 inches) wheelbase for a 'KM' tipper chassis; a higher payload for the 'HA' vans, increased from 8 to 10 cwt; and Mark II 466 cu.in. Bedford diesel having three different power output versions.

In early 1973 the Post Office reviewed their fleet and placed an order for 3,200 'HA' vans. Vauxhall's export market increased when the Bedford began to send 'CF' van models to West Germany, which was considered to be a difficult market to break into.

During the early part of 1973 a new truck model series had just left the drawing board and, satisfied with the development and testing, preparation for production commenced. A £25M project was raised to increase the size of the truck plant at Dunstable where the new truck series would be accommodated. A year later the new series was announced – the 'TM' range. Bedford had now become a member of the heavy brigade.

The introduction was carried out in three phases. At the 1974 Commercial Motor Show eight 'TM' models were released from 16 to 32 tons gross weights, powered by the Detroit Diesel 6V-71 engine. The newly styled 'D' type cab was also offered in three stages; the standard, the full width model 'F' type, and the sleeper cab model 'M' type.

The next phase of introduction of the 'TM' was in mid-1975 with nine more chassis models between 16 and 24 tons gross weights, and a new Bedford diesel engine, the 500, available for the lighter end of the range. In 1976 the new series was completed with eleven more model versions accommodating the wide cab and the sleeper cab, thus taking Bedford into the 42 tonnes (metric tons) market. These latest additions were powered by a larger Detroit Diesel, a V8 cylinder, the 8V-71.

The 'TM' premium quality heavies provided the top-weight 'flagship' models for the range and lifted the name into Europe's highest weight class for the first time. A total of over forty models for the rigid drawbar trailer or articulated operation spanned gross weights from 16260 kgs (16 tons or 35840 lb) to a special 44 tonnes for the Italian market.

Rigid TM truck 4x2 with drawbar trailer. Gross train weight 32 tons

KG box van, 1975. Rated at 12.35 tons GVW

Another addition to the Bedford range was the 16260 kgs (16 ton) gross vehicle weight four wheel drive 'TM' variant developed for military, as well as civilian, use, joining the lighter 'M' type as an extension of Bedford's 'Go anywhere' vehicles. Due for production towards the end of 1976, the 'TM 4-4',as it was designated, had already gained a contract for over 2,000 units, worth £40M, from the British Ministry of Defence.

At the 1976 Commercial Motor Show a van derivative of the new Vauxhall 'Chevette', named the 'Chevanne', was included in the Bedford stand. It was an attractive ½ ton payload van with the style and comfort of its base saloon car. Also exhibited at the Show were a prototype for a four wheel drive CF van for use with ambulance bodies and improvements to the CF range, including the introduction of the General Motors designed 2.1 litre diesel engine as an optional power unit.

All this hard work brought Bedford to outsell all other trucks makes in the United Kingdom in 1976, while in the previous year they had been proclaimed Britain's top export truck makers, despatching over 70% of Dunstable's production overseas.

In 1978 Vauxhall Motors' forward thinking on long haulage, maximum weight trucks was expressed in a 'concept vehicle', the star of the exhibition on the Bedford stand at the National Exhibition Centre, International Motor Show on 20 October. The Bedford design studio had been given a clear objective – 'to create a vehicle of ultra-high specification with a special emphasis on fuel economy, safety, security and comfort for a one-man operation over the longest trunk routes now covered anywhere in the world'. The result, after seventeen months work, was a truck driver's dream, based on the current Bedford TM4200, sixwheeler tractor,

TM sixwheeler
24 tons GVW
with brewer's
stake float
body

Chevanne,
1976

30 tonne
sixwheeler
double drive.

TM tipper
with cab
safety shield,
1976

with luxuriously equipped cab and outstandingly handsome styling. The project had already passed through several phases, including a group of representative drivers and operators for their comments, which had been embodied in the latest vehicle.

The starting point had been the toughest 42 tonner on the market. Two main areas of development attracted the designers' attention; the external aerodynamics to save fuel consumption and a vast improvement in the interior of the Bedford sleeper cab to provide a real home-from-home for the driver: this latter area would relieve the driver from boredom when away from home for some time.

Travelling long distances on haulage work on international motorways, reduced drag is an important factor in fuel economics. This is more apparent with articulated combinations with square fronted containers or box van bodies on semi-trailers. After extensive wind tunnel testing on large scale models to keep the drag factor low, five features were recognised as very relevant to improve aerodynamics. These were –

1. a raised roof incorporating an adjustable air deflector, the theory of which is that when the tractor unit is running solo the air deflector is lowered to roof level, but when the tractor unit is coupled to a semi-trailer with a container or box van body the deflector is raised hydraulically to the appropriate angle to deflect the air-stream over the top of the semi-trailer body.

2. a skirt below the front bumper to reduce the gap to the ground to a minimum. This, however, must be compatible with the practical approach angle.

3. hinged side deflectors up to the height of the cab, filling the gap between the rear of the cab and the front of the semi-trailer. Windtunnel testing suggested considerable scope is here for reducing the turbulence in this gap caused by the running at an angle to the apparent wind, which it is believed is not uncommon on motorways, especially if the roadway lies at right angles to the prevailing winds. Spring loaded stays flush against the semi-trailer body sides and the deflectors also have rubber trailing edges to allow for sharp turns.

4. panniers running the full length of the tractor sides and extensions to wheel-arch covers to help reduce spray from the wheels in wet road conditions.

5. air foils mounted on the windscreen door pillars to minimise dirt deposits on side windows and rear view mirrors.

Military version 4x4, TM 1977

Model KE 10 ton GVW, with platform truck body. The base of the vehicle is the TK

The Bedford designers sat down to consider what could be done to the 'M' type sleeper cab to help the long distance driver to be more self sufficient and ease his journey on long continental hauls. They came up with –

§ Immediate access to a central cold box, as well as a lockable document case and the command of radio/stereo cassette player providing entertainment whilst the driver is at the wheel.

§ When off duty, the driver could draw water from an eight gallon tank through a purifier, so that the tank could be replenished from any water source; wash in a sink with hot and cold water on tap, with an electric shaving point adjacent; cook food from a fridge-freezer in a 3 minute microwave oven; eat at a folding table, on a swivelling upholstered seat.

§ Electricity was chosen for all the extra equipment to avoid the complication of carrying a secondary fuel supply; a 24 volt diesel powered auxiliary generator and additional batteries were housed in the right hand side pannier, opposite the fuel tanks. The generator panel, fridge-freezer, oven and water tank fitted neatly below the traverse bunk, leaving room at its head for a full length wardrobe.

The high cab roof housing the deflector, shroud and air conditioner unit also concealed additional lockable storage space. To enhance the driver's working environment, as well as improve comfort and quiet, dark blue velour nylon upholstery on a sprung driver's seat was matched with heavy extra carpeting and trim.

Extra lighting was provided inside the cab using fluorescence light units mounted above the header panel rail. Driving/fog lamps with protection grilles and the headlamps were recessed into the air dam below the front bumper. Finally, continental-type marker lamps were located in the extremities of the air conditioner intake grille and powerful air horns were fitted on the roof top.

The power unit for the 'Long Haul' was the standard TM4200 tractor unit by Detroit Diesel 8V-71, two stroke engine developing 296 b.h.p (316 P.S.) nett.

The 'Long Haul' caused a great deal of interest at the N.E.C.Show, but there was one snag: the 'TM-Long Haul' was not for sale, although comments were welcome from operators and experienced long distance drivers. The ultra model never went into production in the described form. However, every one of the special features pointed the way to truck design for the future.

***

Military. M type 4x4 (basic TK) with float and full tilt faces big brother TM 4x4 with platform truck body and loading crane

1978 was another memorable year and another milestone in the forty-seven years of Bedford commercial vehicles when, in early October, the total production passed the three million mark. This remarkable output was made up, in round figures, by two million trucks and one million vans. The occasion was celebrated as a central theme of the Bedford stand at the N.E.C. International Motor Show.

Like all motor manufacturers Vauxhall had to improve their Bedford range to maintain their share of the market. It was not always the mechanicals that required improving, but a lot of attention was paid by the public to new looks and improvements in the driver's environment. Now was the time to look at the CF series. First, a new look interior for the 80s with more comfort. A car type design of instrument panel and facia panel for instant and comprehensive reading and giving immediate warning of the vehicle's malfunction. Minor controls were grouped to fall more readily to hand. By the addition of a second steering-column-mounted stalk, the two speed windscreen wiper and washer controls came within finger tip reach from the steering wheel, conforming with the existing controls for the direction indicators, horn and headlight dip. The deep shelf, running the full width of the passenger side, could be hinged into a vertical position to assist engine access through the central cover in the cab. Face-level ventilation, a new style of steering wheel, improved seat trim and improved moulded floor all added to the driver comfort package. The overall versatility of the van range was extended by the introduction of listed options, such as sliding side doors for loading cargo, as opposed to the hinged pattern and this greatly assisted in loading and unloading in confined spaces. Externally the latest range of 'CF' was unchanged for the eighties, the new version appearing at the Frankfurt Show on the General Motors stand. The

TM short wheelbase 16 tonne being exported to Sudan for sugar refinery work

new interior, coupled with the van's widely praised ride, handling and performance, was designed to further increase the appeal of the 'CF', not only as a high specification delivery vehicle, but as a basis for leisure and personnel carrying models, where passenger car driving environment had particular attraction.

On 29th February, 1980, Vauxhall announced a new diesel engine range for Bedford vehicles, naming it the 'Blue Series'. Initially, the development was a 8.2 litre six cylinder, in-line direct injection diesel engine developing 202 b.h.p (151 kW) for use in military vehicles. This engine became the base of a naturally aspirated version developing 128 b.h.p (95kW) for the Bedford 'TK' series and another developing 151 b.h.p. (112 kW) for the 'TM' series. The Cummins diesels

Development vehicle of the super trucks, articulated tractor unit, complete with aerofoils, 1983

47

and the Detroit Diesel engines were maintained for the heavier end of the 'TM' series.

Vauxhall continued with their development of the commercial vehicle range during the 1980s, analysing the market and carefully watching their main competitor, Ford. Ford had shot ahead with high truck sales, encouraging Vauxhall to further advance by the introduction of the 'TL' range Bedford in May, 1980. The 'TL' was Britain's first new medium truck for the eighties. Low cost maintenance, new high levels of cab comfort and smooth good looking lines in styling were the leading features for the new series. It was introduced with a tilt design cab, making a major contribution to extending Bedford's appeal in this category.

However, the model 'TK' was retained, offering the operator a choice between the new tilt cab concept or continue with the sound existing range. Mechanically the 'TL' range used thoroughly tried and tested components, commonising with the 'TK': with this combination Bedford claimed to offer an unbeatable non-HGV range. The new tilt cab offered a roomy, luxurious and ergonomically planned work place for the driver. It could be tilted through 50°, exposing the whole of the engine compartment and providing ample clearance for maintenance and the removal of the engine if considered necessary for major overhauls; it was considered by the engineers that generous access by means of hinged valances in the rear quarter panels of the cab gave sufficient room for all routine servicing to be carried out without disturbing the cab. This access for routine servicing was the same as that provided for the TK series.

To ensure adequate power for the variety of applications in which the TL could be employed internationally the model range specifications included five Bedford power units – three diesel and two petrol engines. For the middleweight truck applications demanding extra high power levels, such as in some European markets where drawbar trailer operation is common or in high speed long distance solo operation, Bedford extended the installation of the 'Blue Series' larger diesels as an alternative power unit for the 7.5, 9 and 10.2 tonne gross weight TL chassis with an engine rated version of 128 b.h.p (95 kW). The 'Blue Series' engine gave extra power increasing the powerweight ratio factor by between 25 and 30%, as compared with the standard power units.

The remainder of the specified power units for the TL series is
* The 'Blue Series' 8.2 litre diesel rated at the higher rate of 150 b.h.p (112kW), installed in the 14.7 and 16.3 tonnes gross weight models.
* The 'Blue Series' diesel at the lower rate of 128 b.h.p (95kW), installed in the 19.3 tonne gross combination weight model TL1930 tractor unit, also available in the 12.5 tonne gross weight model TL1260 chassis.

Bedford's 330, 524 litre six cylinder diesel engine rated at 98 b.h.p. (73 kW) was offered for the 7.5 to 12.5 tonne gross weight and the 16.3 ton gross combination weight tractor units. Bedford's 220, 3.6 litre four cylinder diesel engine rated at 65 b.h.p (48.5 kW) was offered for the 5.7 and 7.5 tonne gross weight level. The introduction of the Bedford diesel engine did not mean the phasing out of the Bedford petrol engine, which was retained for domestic customers where petroleum fuel was essential and for overseas countries where diesel fuel is at a premium or rare. Bedford's 300 4.9 litre six cylinder petrol engine rated at 114 b.h.p (84.5 kW) was offered for the same range of TL models as the 330 Bedford diesel, while Bedford's 214 3.5 litre six cylinder petrol engine rated

TM 4x4 civilian
version with waste
disposal unit body,
1980

Model TM sixwheeler double
drive.
Heavy duty tipper. Steel body.
Powered by the Detroit-Diesel 6V-71 engine

S series
7 ton chassis
on the
assembly line

at 83 b.h.p (62 kW) was for the 5.7 and 7.5 tonnes gross weight models.

The choice of standard wheelbases for the TL ranged from 2.92 metres (115 inches) to 5.69 metres (224 inches), permitting body lengths from 3.4 metres (132 inches) to 6.7 metres (264 inches). The drive line was through either the Bedford four speed, Turner five speed or Eaton five speed gearboxes. Choice of gearboxes was available for the TL models up to 12.5 tonnes gross weight: above that five speed with either wide ratio or overdrive types was the standard choice. The final drive was by Bedford's single speed rear axle with a wide range of axle ratios to suit the operations, however, two speed rear axles were optional for models above the 9 tonne weight.

One of the main objectives laid down for the TL range was the 'ride comfort': new standards in driver comfort were gained substantially from the new smooth-riding tapered leaf front suspension. The exceptional length of these springs at 1.8 metres (71 inches) was a major factor in promoting good ride characteristics, aided by the reduction of interleaf friction which was possible with the two tapered leaves. This suspension design also brought lower stresses and gave greater mass of main leaf metal to resist roll and wind-up during braking, as well as having better compliance with road surfaces, thus improving handling and road holding. Further chassis engineering refinements for the TL includes hydraulic assistance for the operation of the clutch for all models, corrosion-resistant reinforced plastic piping, flexible waterproof convolute nylon sleeving to protect electric wiring and smooth action power assisted recirculating ball steering gear. Dual air-hydraulic braking extended to the lightest models and all models had the spring-brake fail safe parking brake.

In June, 1980, a light pick-up truck, offering good cargo space with a high performance and economy, joined the Bedford commercials, designated as the KB26 and this made Vauxhall a strong contender in the growing market for pick-ups in the 1 ton load category. The KB26 was manufactured by General Motors' associated company in Japan, Isuzu Motors, Ltd. The pick-up was a very well proven vehicle with over half a million sold world wide. This was a blow against the British motor industry and British designers, but demonstrated the problem of being part of a global multi-national organisation.

The 1.6 litre petrol engine featured a single overhead camshaft and cross flow cylinder head, the engine developing 79 b.h.p at 5400 r.p.m, with a noticeably lively performance. With a wheelbase of 2.995 metres (118 inches) and a wide track of 1.34 metres (52.8 inches) the KB26 had a payload of 1200 kgs (2640 lb) with a comparatively large cargo area. Designed with a ladder type chassis frame with rigid box section sidemembers, cross braced at six points, on which was mounted an all steel cab and truck float body. It had independent wish-bone front suspension with torsion bar springs and an anti-roll bar. The semi-elliptical longitudinal rear suspension had six leaves, supplemented with double acting hydraulic shock absorbers. It had a turning circle of 12.4 metres (40 feet). Finally, front disc and rear drum brakes were hydraulically operated with servo assistance.

Unveiled at the U.K. Motor Show in mid-October, 1980, was Bedford's new advanced truck aerodynamics for their latest concept vehicle, known as the 'TL Aero'. This exercise was an extension of the experimental work on the 'TM Long Haul' tractor unit designed for long distances heavyweight haulage. Whilst based on the 'TL' middleweight truck chassis, this fresh research was applied round the

TM 1700 truck, long wheelbase 4x2 forward control with drawbar trailer, 2 axle type. 32 tons gross train weight, 1974

cab and bodywork on the practical application of aerodynamics: the airflow was smoothed over and around the front and then controlled air movement over the rest of the vehicle, reducing projected spray and providing space for a sleeper cab compartment plus storage space along its sides and over the cab. A built in under--ride barrier was provided at the rear and this, together with enclosing panels, and rear mounted side and roof foils, further reduced turbulent air-flow over the vehicle.

A spoiler was built-in below the front bumper, incorporating retractable driving lights. The roof panel carried a deflector which, for non-fixed bodies such as containers, or when running as a flat platform truck, can be adjusted through a vertical range of 305 mm (12 inches). Vertical flash side panels were installed at the rear of the cab to bridge the gap between the cab and the body. As well as smoothing air-flow along the sides of the vehicle, these panels also concealed the cab sleeper compartment in a rearward extension of the top part of the cab. Above the sleeper compartment and behind the roof deflector, there was a storage space for the canvas tilt or other bulky items, and below there were compartment each side containing the engine air-intake and tool box. The outer faces of these lower compartments also acted as air-flow devices, providing an outlet for the air directed under the cab.

The lower sides of the truck rearwards from the front wheels were fitted with rubber skirts as part of the 'air management' package and above these on both sides were mounted flush panniers with quick release access panels - two giving access to the fuel tank and the battery and other chassis components and two providing additional storage space. At the extreme ends of the vehicle sides were mounted vertical air-foils, complemented by a horizontal foil across the width of the roof. Even the under-ride barrier at the rear of the vehicle, primarily installed for the safety of motorists, had a dual function. The barrier comprised two energy absorbing foils as part of the panelled-in rear of the vehicle, acting as the final element in the direction of the air-flow. The under-ride also acts as a 'stop' warning actuator when reversing up to loading bays.

Driver comfort got the full treatment in the Aero. The refined new 'TL' cab was equipped with multi-adjacent 'posture' driver's seat. Between the driver and passenger seat was a control console incorporating storage tray and document pocket, while a centrally mounted roof module provided a full range of stereo and radio facilities together with spot lights. General cab illumination was provided by concealed fluorescent tubes in the rear door pillars. The cab area had been extended rearwards at the level of the parcel shelf, itself re-modelled with extra compartments and, at night, the vertically parked bunk bed hinged down over the shelf. Privacy, when asleep on the foam-mattress bed, was provided by a concealed roller blind pulled down from a housing in the roof panel.

To keep abreast of the latest technology in the design of low loaders for the distribution services Bedford employed rubber suspension. The first model fitted with this was exhibited at the National Exhibition Centre – Motor Show in 1982; a 16 tonne gross weight model, the TL 1630 chassis cab. This was expected to attract the close interest of transport managers, particularly those responsible for the multidrop deliveries ranging from soft drinks to coal: those who would benefit from the exceptionally low loading height of only 914 mm (36 inches). Developed by Norde, introduced on the TL 1630 as a Special Vehicle Option as an alternative to the conventional semi-elliptic leaf steel springs.

The advantage of progressively stiffening suspension medium, an inherent characteristic of rubber, is the high degree of suspension control and, especially, good stability with high centre of gravity. The rubber suspension was also fail safe and quiet in operation, which were two beneficial environmental aspects. Durability was claimed for over half a million miles under average operating conditions. The low height feature of the vehicle was significantly improved by several inches compared with the conventional leaf spring suspension, enabling the vehicle to meet the criteria expected by the operators for low loader vehicles. The 16 tonne distribution truck was powered by the 'Blue Series' 8.2 litre turbocharged diesel engine, developing 129 kW (173 b.h.p.) at 2500 r.p.m. and the transmission was an Allison MT653 automatic, under special order.

Bedford had completely reconstructed and strengthened its line-up of the 'TM' heavy models to secure an impact in the highly competitive top weight premium truck market in 1982. The considerably extended 'TM' line-up included sixty-two new models designed to meet the requirements of both domestic and export sales.

To take care of the United Kingdom market twenty-six models were announced, – twelve tractors, 4 x 2; four 6 x 2; four 6 x 4 rigid six wheelers; and six 4 x 2 rigid four wheelers. The new 'TM' trucks and tractor units provided a substantially wider choice of engines, transmissions and rear axles. In particular special emphasis had been placed on providing additional variants for higher gross weight of up to 44 tonnes, with a corresponding increase in power outputs up to 387 b.h.p. The 'TM' premium quality heavies were the top-weight 'Flagship' models for the Bedford range and had lifted the make into Europe's highest weight class for the first time since the 'TM' was launched in 1974. The latest generation of fuel efficiency drive-lines gave the operator an economical, high performance durable

TL 1000. Middleweight truck series, chassis cab, 1982

haulage vehicle.

There were new tractors at 36.5 and 44 tonnes gross combination weights, new 6 x 2 and 6 x 4 sixwheeler rigid trucks at 26 tonnes gross vehicle weight and up to 44 tonnes gross train weight, new 4 x 2 trucks at 17 and 19 tonnes gross vehicle weights, with train weights also up to 44 tonnes. To power these models Bedford had introduced new engines alongside the well-proven Detroit Diesel 6V-71, which included the Detroit Diesel 6V-92 and the 8V-92 'Silver Series', with turbocharged after coolers and three Cummins diesel engines, the E235, E290 and E370 models.

The success of the drive line was due to the careful selection of transmissions and rear axles together with the appropriate power units. Nine speed gearboxes were standard with all engines under 300 b.h.p., with the exception of the 6 x 4 sixwheeler with the Cummins engines, which had thirteen speed gearboxes. The models with the Detroit diesels – 6V-92TA developed 313 b.h.p; 8V-92TA developed 387 b.h.p; while the Cummins E370 developed 352 b.h.p, transmitting their power through the Eaton-Fuller thirteen speed gearbox. This gearbox was also available as an option to the nine speed unit used with all engines, except the 6V-71. Further options were the Eaton-Fuller 11609 and the 11613 for all TM variants up to and including the Cummins E370. However, the Fuller 14613, with its higher input torque capacity, was used with the Detroit Diesel 8V-92TA.

To continue with the complete drive-line Dana Spicer twin plate 365mm (14 inch) diameter clutch was fitted standard on all models, except those powered by the Cummins E370 diesel and the Detroit Diesel 8V-92, which were equipped with a 394mm (15.5 inch) diameter clutch. All clutches incorporated a feature of automatic adjustment. High capacity Spicer 1760 series propeller shafts were through–

out the range, except for the power unit 8V-92TA line, which needed the higher rated propeller shaft 1810 series. Finally the rear axles: eleven tonne Bedford rear axle was available or there was a choice of a thirteen tonne capacity rear axle, the Eaton 25199 or the Rockwell U180. These Eaton and Rockwell rear axles provided ratios of 3.4:1, 3.7:1 and 4.1:1 and were fitted with a differential lock as standard.

For the sixwheelers the tandem bogie featured the Eaton DS400 double drive, but for vehicles using the higher power diesel unit, 8V-92TA, the higher capacity tandem unit, the Eaton DS480, was necessary. The efficient drive-line configuration specified for the TM low revving engines from the direct drive transmissions and single reduction rear axles was complemented by using premium tread tyres and fitted as standard, offering lower rolling resistance and improved tyre wear.

New models had been added to the TM range and were available in various wheelbases, including new standard models capable of accepting the mounting of bodies up to 9 metres (354.3 inches) on 4 x 2 and 6 x 2 models and up to 7.6 metres (200.2 inches) on 6 x 4 models. To cater for the increased gross weights it was essential to increase the strength of the chassis frames, first to accommodate increases in gross combination weights and then train weights and, secondly, to cater for the new wheelbases. With the number of frames now at seventy, it was essential to rationalise and a programme was set up to reduce the potential number to twenty, achieved by engineering frames to take a greater number of mechanical installations.

The suspension was improved by making use of the material: the rear suspension comprised four parabolic taper leaf spring pack for use with the thirteen tonne capacity rear axle and three parabolic taper leaf spring pack with the eleven tonne rear axle capacity.

With the EEC regulations ever increasing Bedford updated their TM vehicle braking systems, not only for current regulations, but also to cover the EEC proposals on braking. Two line braking system was optional to meet the United

The 'Astra' commercial version of the Vauxhall saloon car of the same name, 1982

Kingdom requirements. The secondary trailer braking system for these models was incorporated with the parking brake valve. To complete the braking, nylon pipes were used throughout to avoid corrosion, braking reservoirs had to be rationalised both in number and in method of installation. For ease of access the reservoirs had to be regrouped in one location and repositioned on the outside of the chassis frame side members. Finally, in addition a Bendix Westinghouse air-dryer installation was made available as a regular production option.

Many aspects of the chassis componentry on the TM had been revised to improve the overall refinement of the truck range. Four basic fuel tanks were offered in various capacities; 170 litre (37.4 gallons), 250 litres (58.3 g.), 340 litres (74.8 g.) and 410 litres (90.2 g.). To accommodate these tanks the spare wheel carrier had to be relocated to the rear of the chassis frame.

Standard electrics catered for cold-start and for winter conditions down to -25°. Halogen headlamps on all models and a new rear lamp cluster incorporating tail, stop, reverse and fog lamps in one assembly were adopted.

To improve semi-trailer swing clearance in articulated combinations the Donaldson air-intake stack and separator had to be repositioned outwards with the air cleaner mounted horizontally for most models.

The sleeper cab was made available more widely on most new TM models and a full range of optional equipment was obtainable with the addition of more regular production options. Production of the latest TM concept was already on the assembly line which was commissioned in 1980.

On 17th March, 1982, half a million TJ had been produced, a range first introduced in 1958, with success still endorsed by overseas sales worth somewhere around £50 million a year. The TJ had been sold in over 150 countries, with exports representing a vast majority of 90% of the half million built.

Despite the deepening of the recession and the variable strength of the pound in the early eighties, 8,354 TJs were shipped to 35 different countries in 1981, mostly in KD (knocked down) kit form for overseas assembly. Since its introduction the TJ had captured a significant share of the overseas truck markets including Pakistan, Bangladesh, Malaysia, Sudan and many other parts of Africa. The highest African sales had been in Nigeria, where Bedford remained the market leader, commanding one third of the truck sales in the 2 to 10 ton range. Federated Motor Industries (FMI) of Nigeria had assembled models for some twenty-one years from kits supplied from Bedford's Dunstable plant and a record production figure of 640 vehicles was announced by FMI for the month of February, 1982, the majority being TJ models. Since the normal control TJ range had been introduced improvements and development of mechanicals had taken place, the 1982 line-up including some seventeen basic variants covering weights from 3.5 to 11 tons, with a choice of two petrol and two diesel engines.

Many four wheel drive vehicles have been marketed in the U.K. and overseas based on the marketing instinct of one-make fleets, providing better servicing and spares, many common, keeping dealers' stocks to a workable variety. On 4th June, 1982, Vauxhall Motors developed a four-wheel drive pick-up, designated as the KB41. This new model further extended the line-up of Bedford's 'go anywhere' models, a selection which included the premium duty TM 4 x 4 and the ubiquitous M type. Typical applications expected to be fulfilled were in farming, the public utilities, the building trade, site construction, etc., in fact, a host of differing roles

'Astra' vans. Featuring choice of petrol or diesel engines, 1982

where off-road capabilities are often an essential requirement. But, once again, the KB41 was manufactured by G.M.C.'s associated company, Isuzu Motors, Ltd., of Japan: another indication of light models being taken away from the British designers.

The KB41 had a choice of both petrol and diesel engines, independent suspension, self-adjusting brake, and four-wheel synchromesh gearbox. The four wheel drive was achieved via a two speed transfer gearbox with a low ratio of 1.87:1 and a high ratio in direct drive. When the terrain varies from rough to smooth a special features of the model was the ability in high ratio to switch from four wheel drive to two wheel drive and back again without having to stop, with an indicator light confirming that the vehicle was in all wheel drive. A wheelbase of 2.65 metres (104 inches) was shorter than the KB26, 4 x 2 truck, and a gross vehicle weight of 2350 kgs (5181.75 lb) provided a payload of 1000 kgs (2205 lb).

The launch of the KB41 coincided with an extensive month-long tour of Bedford on/off road vehicles under the banner of 'Bedford Overlanders' to demonstrate to specialist operators the capabilities of this type of vehicle when operating under arduous off-road conditions.

With the introduction of the new, higher-powered variants of the Bedford 3.6 and 5.4 litre 'Red Series' turbocharged diesel engines, Bedford went into 1983 model year featuring quiet, powerful turbocharged engines as standard across the board. The naturally aspirated engine continued to be available for non-European export markets. The 3.6 litre, 4 cylinder, developed 64.9 kW (87 b.h.p) at 2600 r.p.m. and replaced the existing 72 b.h.p. turbocharged unit for the light truck variants: the 5.4 litre, six cylinder, developed 100.8 kW (135 b.h.p.) at 2600 r.p.m.

For the 1983 production cabs had been extensively revised, new trim and seating for the 'TL' middleweights and even more substantial changes for the 'TM' heavies in internal appearance, comfort and convenience. Axles for the middleweight were redesigned and the use of gearboxes featuring 'multi-contact' meshing had been extended on the 'TM' range. Drive line improvements were made to cater for the new power units for the 'TL' and 'TK', irrespective of the power unit specified. Bedford rear axles for 5.5 and to 8.5 tonne models featured a new larger diameter crown wheel and pinion, while other internal changes gave improved oil circulation and reduced frothing. The then current 11 tonne Bedford heavy-duty spiral bevel gear axle used on the 15/16 tonne chassis had been modified to a hypoid bevel gear design. The new Bedford axle replaced proprietary units on Bedford powered 'TM' chassis. Differential locks were available as an option. Additional rear axle ratios of 3.89:1 and 6.8:1 on medium range axles enabled the overdrive gearboxes to be replaced by more efficient direct top boxes, both four and five speed without sacrificing top gear performance.

In January the 'TM' range of engines had an addition, the introduction of the Cummins L10, 10 litre, six cylinder in-line 250 b.h.p. diesel. Four new 'TM's were introduced, two 'TM3250' tractor units and two 'TM2600' rigid trucks. With the major restructuring announced in 1983, together with the latest packing of cab improvements and drive train requirements, this represented the world's most competitive heavy-duty truck ranges.

A light front wheel drive Bedford delivery van, combining highly practical load carrying capacity with advanced standards of passenger comfort – the Astra van – made its debut on 11th October, 1982. It provided over 0.5 tonne payload capacity and replaced the Chevanne, being offered alongside the 'HA' range. The Astra van extended the top end of the light van market to meet the needs of business people looking for the advanced stylish image it projected. The power unit was transversely installed and it had a 1.3 litre petrol or 1.6 litre diesel engine, developing 75 b.h.p (DIN) at 5800 r.p.m. or 54 b.h.p. (DIN) respectively, a four speed gearbox standard with G.M. Automatic transmission available for both petrol and diesel. There was a fuel tank capacity of 50 litres (11 gallons) for both petrol and diesel.

The Astra van provided a usable volume of 63.9 cu.ft. for payload capacity at a weight of over 0.5 tonnes. Wheelbase was 2.514 metres (99 inches) and wheel track 1.4 metres (55 inches). It had front independent suspension, McPherson struts and coil springs; the rear suspension was compound crank trailing arm with Minibloc progressive coil spring. A transverse torsion beam at the rear, telescopic hydraulic shock absorbers and front and rear anti-roll bars were fitted as standard to give firmly controlled ride comfort and stability in all conditions. The brakes were hydraulically operated; disc front, drum rear, dual circuit servo assisted.

A Bedford dealer of Alkobhar, Saudi Arabia, Mohammed Faleh Al-Hajri Establishment, placed an order for ten special articulated 60 tonne gross combination weight tractor units for long distance haulage over the Middle Eastern routes. The tractor was a Bedford extra heavy sixwheeler tractor unit. The first machine, designated the 'TM6000', of the £360,000 deal delivered was exhibited at the Jeddah Motor Show, 28th November–4th December, 1982.

Bedford engineers designed and developed the new 'TM6000' tractor to haul a gross weight of up to 60 tonnes, with an off-the-road capability, using the existing 'TM4400', 44 tonnes gross combination weight, as a basis. The new tractor joined the much revised and strengthened line-up of 'TM's announced earlier in 1982, demonstrating Bedford's policy of developing specifications closely tailored to individual operator's requirements.

The 'TM6000' was powered by the turbocharged and after-cooled Detroit Diesel 6V-92TA 'Silver Series' engine developing 233 kW (312.2 b.h.p.) at 2100 r.p.m. with a torque capacity of 1264 Nm (931.6 lbft) at 1300 r.p.m. Drive line was through the Fuller RT11609A, 9 speed direct top constant mesh gearbox via a twin plate 394mm (15.5 inch) diameter clutch to a double drive tandem GKN (Kirkstall) D66 single speed, spiral bevel gear drive hub reduction axles, rated at 22 tonnes. It had an 18.4 tonne capacity front axle. The GKN (Kirkstall) D80 tandem bogie capacity of 26 tonnes was specified for rigids. Air operated inter-axle and leading cross axle differential locks provided extra traction in extreme conditions. Large diameter 588mm (24 inch) cast steel demountable Trilex wheels were fitted as standard equipment for maximum brake cooling and increased ground clearance, shod with Michelin F24 tyres.

Suspension was changed from the equipment used on the 'TM4400', replacing the parabolic taper leaf springs by semi-elliptic multi-leaf spring, which were already specified as optional equipment on the 'TM4400'. The rear suspension was replaced by the Hendrickson 'balance beam' two spring suspension.

To carry the load a new flat topped ladder type frame assembly, incorporating high tensile steel-alloy frame sidemembers, was adopted, with dimensions of 300 mm (11.8 inches) deep, 8 mm (0.31 inches) web thickness and 14 mm (0.55 inches) deep flanges: this gave exceptional strength, eliminating the need for flitching. Standard equipment included 340 litre (75 gallon) fuel tanks. The kerb weight was 9483 kgs (20900 lb) and distributed loads were front axle 4948 kgs (10900 lb) and rear bogie 4535 kgs (10000 lb). The wheelbase was 3.96 metres (156 inches). The weights included spare wheel and fuel, but not the fifth wheel coupling. The 'TM6000' was equipped with the full width sleeper cab, generously appointed to a high level of specification, comprising the latest requirements introduced on the 'TM' cabs for 1983.

One range seemingly left in the background whilst the concentration was employed on the heavies, was the 'CF' van and light truck range. However, they had not been forgotten as development had been moving towards major advances in refined engineering, making the latest 'CF' range a fundamentally different van for 1983. One of the main benefits was the reduction of interior noise levels and other objectives included better driver comfort, improved ride and electronic ignition for greater combustion efficiency. Through a series of improvements to reduce noise generation at source, interior noise levels in the new 'CF' had been reduced by 6dBA, which represents a reduction of no less than one third in

Model CF350 3.5 tonne, equipped with a 3 way tipper body, 1982

58

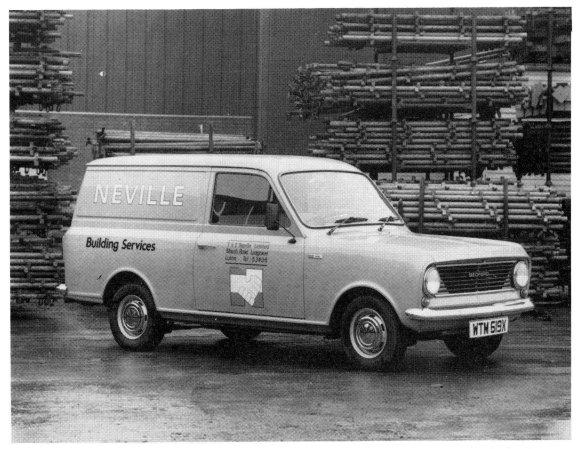

perceived noise or loudness. In terms of refinement the interior of the 'CF' came close to passenger car standards and was certainly one of the quietest vehicles in its class. Resulting improvements comprised new spring mounting featuring revised front and rear spring eyes and redesigned larger diameter rubber bushes to help isolate drive-line noise. Engine and drive line mounts were considered for attention and had been improved to reduce the transmission of mechanically generated vibration.

The underside of the body had been coated with bituminous underbody sealing compound and the application of this floor damping material resulted in reduction of general noise and, as well as cutting noise levels, greatly improved corrosion resistance.

Single tyre equipped models had multi-leaf variable rate springs at the rear, allied with new designed damper settings and revised spring rates for the independently sprung front wheels.

Front axle plated weights for the short wheel base, CF230 and CF250 petrol models, increased to 1130 kgs (2491.6 lb) from 1020 kgs (2249 lb) by fitting the heavy duty springs already used on the corresponding diesel models.

THE PUBLIC SERVICE VEHICLE MARKET

The first Bedford chassis specially built for the public service vehicle market appeared in the August of 1931, some five months after Bedford's first vehicle. This was a 2 ton truck chassis modified in line with the Ministry of Transport vehicle regulations affecting Public Service Vehicles. Designated as the model WB series, the WHB had a short wheelbase of 3.327 metres (131 inches) and the WLB was a long wheelbase of 3.98 metres (157 inches). The WHB was suitable for 14 seater bus and coach bodies, while the WLB was for 20 seaters. The price was right – £250 and £265 for the WHB and WLB chassis respectively. However, Bedford based buses had appeared before the introduction of the WHB and WLB, as early as July, 1931. The body builders Jennings of Sandbach offered a 20 seater passenger vehicle body for mounting on the long wheelbase model 2 ton goods chassis, and another body builder, Rainforth of Lincoln, delivered a 20 seater on a modified 2 ton chassis to an operator in Mareham-le-Fen, Lincolnshire: this latter could safely be regarded as Bedford's first operating bus. At the end of August, 1931, a 14 seater bus body was built and mounted by Waveney of Oulton Broad on a short wheelbase chassis and delivered to an operator at Melchbourne, near Bedford, becoming known as the Melchbourne Flyer, operating daily until 1964.

The models WHB and WLB chassis had similar mechanicals as their truck counterparts. Fitted with the Bedford six cylinder 3.177 litre petrol engine developing 44 b.h.p. at 2400 r.p.m., rated power under the RAC formula at 26.33 h.p. Drive line was through a four speed gearbox to a spiral bevel gear driven rear axle; similar drive to the truck chassis. The rear axle ratio was 5.8:1. A generous turning circle of 17.3 metres (57 feet) for the long wheelbase was acceptable. Other body builders joined in supplying bus and coach bodies for mounting on these two chassis.

It was amazing, as a newcomer to the P.S.V. market, that in the last quarter of 1931 52% of all 14 and 20 seater buses and coaches registered in the United Kingdom were Bedford. Exports began to find their way from the Luton plant before the end of that same year.

Later the short wheelbase, WLB 14 seater, ceased production because the demand was low and did not justify the continuation of production.

In April, 1932, the 12 cwt light delivery van range, models VYC and VXC, based on the Vauxhall 'Cadet' saloon car, was introduced and these model chassis attracted attention as a useful base for a seven seater rural bus. This concept strengthened Bedford's entry into the P.S.V. market.

Bedford buses hit the success they deserved, healthy overseas markets being created with Bedford buses appearing in New Zealand, Sierra Leone, Egypt, Denmark, Sweden, Jamaica, Spain, Belgium, Argentine, China and several other countries. On the domestic market sales were also booming: by the end of 1932 Bedford had claimed 62% of the 8 to 20 seater bus and coach market – and this was just the beginning.

In November, 1933, the new 3 ton chassis was unveiled at the London Commercial Motor Show, the model range WT, with semi-forward control and short

(Above) 20 seater collecting miners at the Ebbw Vale Colliery, 1931
(Right) Duple 20 seater on the WLB chassis. Coach running between Burnley and Barley, Lancashire

Melchbourne Flyer. Waveney built body, 14 seater on WHB chassis

61

Duple bodied 20 seater. The Plymouth operator called the Bedford, 'Far and away the best 20 seater on the market', 1931

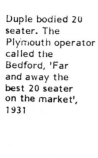

38/40 seater school bus by Duple on WLB chassis (Below) Duple 20 seater, sunsaloon coach, 1932

A 14 seater and a 20 seater in 1932 averaging 1,000 miles a week each. Operator Forman Bros of Coatbridge

bonnet providing another basis for an enterprising bus market for up to 26 passengers with comfortable operating conditions.

The new public service vehicle, the model WTB, was introduced in 1935. This had a wheelbase of 4.24 metres (167 inches) and was powered by the proven six cylinder 26.33 h.p. petrol engine used on the earlier goods models. Designed to accommodated 26 passengers, the model remained in production until 1939. Its popularity eventually accounted for 55% of the British bus and coach market. Duple Bodies of Hendon gave birth to their first 'Vista' 25 seater luxurious coach body on the Bedford WTB chassis, but before the WTB had been announced, Duple and other body builders were already constructing P.S.V. bodies for mounting on the model WT 3 ton chassis. Duple Motor Bodies really 'went to town' with coach bodies on the newly introduced WTB chassis; in fact, as early as 1935, there was a choice of five different Duple bodies mounted on WTB – a 'bus-cum-coach', two models of the De-Lux coach and two of the 'Super De-Lux' Touring Coach. The cheapest was a 20 seater service bus at £625 complete and the dearest a 25 seater K D Super De-Lux coach priced at £785. Money had certainly been put into the body, bearing in mind that the chassis price was £290.

In the summer of 1938 changes were made to the W range, including the WTB. The much improved petrol engine, now at 27.34 h.p., developed 72 b.h.p, increasing the power by 12%, and there was also a slightly modified front radiator grille.

1939 saw the disappearance of the seven seater rural bus, which had enjoyed a long run since 1932, while the WTB was approaching the end of its production. At that time Duple were selling 20 and 26 seater buses, the Hendonian coach, the 'Vista II' and the 'Vista III' Super coaches.

The outbreak of the Second World War put Bedford to war production and the output of buses and coaches ended. At the outbreak of activities small buses and coaches by Bedford accounted for 70% of the models on the roads of the British Isles: quite an achievement for a comparative newcomer to the PSV industry.

Just before the beginning of war Bedford had launched new models, K, M and

The 7 seater Rural Bus was a dual purpose passengers/goods vehicle. On standard 12 cwt van chassis. Disc wheels, 1932. (Below left) Duple 'Vista' 29 seater coach on OB chassis with 174 inch wheelbase. (Below right) WTB 26 seater bus. Based on the forward engined, short bonnet 3 ton long wheelbase chassis of 1935

Arthur Mulliner built coach body. Note strange styling at rear of coach

WTB chassis, short bonnet with Duple 26 seater body. Note the unusual location of the spare wheel, 1935

War time Bedford OWB with bodywork to Ministry of Supply specification Operated by Leeds City Transport. Being overtaken by an AEC Regent double decker (Below) Fleet of Duple service buses for Western Welsh

O ranges, with the K and M models replacing the W type. The O range took Bedford into the 5 ton payload capacity category and this range found a new basis for another bus and coach chassis of 4.42 metres (174 inches) wheelbase, the model OB. The OB had been designed to accommodate a 29 seater bus or coach body, but it could be stretched to take 32 seats.

As the was proceeded and everything was geared to maintaining war supplies no P.S.Vs were being produced. However, in 1941, it was realised by the British government that there was an acute shortage of transport in many parts of the country. Normal civilian transport services were becoming difficult to maintain, resulting in the Ministry of Supply approaching Vauxhall and authorising them to release a number of Bedford bus chassis on to the civilian market: thus the Bedford OB model became the only single deck bus chassis to be produced during the years of war activities. During that period some 3,300 OBs were produced, including some for the armed forces, designated as the model OWB. The bodies were built to a wartime standard; wooden slatted seats, simple jack-knife doors and virtually no trim. The mechanicals were the same as the WTB which it replaced with the power drive of a 28 h.p. six cylinder petrol engine, four speed gearbox and spiral bevel gear driven rear axle.

By May, 1947, the OB was advertised as suitable for 26 and 32 seater coach-work, the chassis price being £495. Although Duple Vista bodies were becoming the standard to be mounted on the OB, other Vista type bodies were built by Longwell Green Coaches of Bristol and the Scottish Motor Traction Company. The model OB was not just a success, but almost became part of the life of the community as one of the best loved small buses and coaches in the British Isles. Wherever one went there were Bedford OBs, in municipal transport, holiday excursions and private coach parties.

Although the OB was Bedford's main P.S.V. in the 1940s, a demand materialised for another chassis to accommodate 20 passengers: to meet this demand the M range truck of 3.36 metres (143 inch) wheelbase modified and shared the same petrol engine and transmission as the OB.

For overseas markets where more ground clearance was necessary because of poor terrain another version of the OB was introduced. The variant was based on the long wheelbase 3.987 metres (157 inches), 3/4 ton chassis, the OL, modified to suit passenger carrying vehicle regulations. Many were exported to Cyprus and ended up with dual purpose bodies - passengers inside and goods on the tailboard and on a large luggage carrier on the roof. The OB production ended in the late

A luxury 20 seater touring coach on OB chassis by Thurgood of Ware. (Right) Hotel bus on M type chassis. 143 inch wheelbase

1950s after over 16,000 chassis had been sold, including the 3,000 wartime OWBs. The OB had become the firm foundation of Vauxhall's P.S.V. business and it was from the popularity of the OBs that the business flourished until the commercial side of Vauxhall ceased production.

1950 was another year for the Commercial Motor Show in London. Exhibited on the Vauxhall stand, among the new 'S' forward control commercial trucks, was the new range of public service vehicles and coaches, the SB series. This had forward control, entirely new design, with longer wheelbase of 5.23 metres (206 inches). The original seating capacity was for 33. Duple were well in the fore for mounting new style bodies on the SB chassis (price £690) – the 'Vega', with a similar capacity Mark IV service bus.

A new power unit, 4.9 litre (300 cu.in) petrol engine developing 110 b.h.p at 3200 r.p.m. with a torque capacity of 234 lbft at 1200 r.p.m was introduced both for the bus/coach chassis and the 'S' goods range vehicles. Within two years the SB had grown; the Duple body was now 2.438 metres (96 inches) wide and lengthened by some 457 mm (18 inches). By the end of 1978 approximately 52,000 SB chassis had been sold, many of them to overseas markets.

In the early 1950s another small P.S.V. chassis, the OLAZ, a modified version of the OL goods chassis with a shorter wheelbase of 3.98 metres (157 inches) and

SB chassis by Duple Bodies of Hendon

SB chassis with a 36 seater Seagull coach by Burlingham of Blackpool

SB chassis by Yeats of Scarborough, the 'Riviera' coach. Heavy chrome plated mouldings adorn the coach body

A rare styled 33 seater by Arlington Motors on SB chassis

'Pay-as-you-enter' service bus by Yeates. The 'Fiesta' had the entrance ahead of the front wheels.

Another SB
Model OLAZ with a Duple Sportsman
body, early 1950s

Duple Vista 29 seater forward
control on a C chassis

powered by the 28 h.p. six cylinder petrol engine was introduced. Later Plaxtons
of Scarborough brought in a 33/35 seater and Duple produced an alternative design
for the front end of the 'Vega', which was exhibited at the Brussels Show in 1953.
Also in 1953 came the first offer of a diesel engine for the Bedford commercials,
a Perkins R6 six cylinder in-line developing 108 b.h.p, available as an option to the
300 cu.in. petrol engine; this diesel became available in the bus and coach chassis.
At the 1953 Scottish Motor Show in Glasgow, five new SB based bus/coaches were
exhibited and on view in the SMT showrooms: these were the Duple new Super
Vega, the Plaxton Venturer, the Riviera by Yeates, the Duple service bus and a
Burlingham luxury coach.

In spite of Ford's efforts to penetrate the market with their quite successful
'R' series and Commer's contribution to the market Bedford still continued as the
leading chassis maker for public service vehicles and gained strength even against
such experienced and long-life coach chassis manufacturers as Leyland.

1955 was another year full of events; April, the first British Coach Rally (with many more to follow, now known as the Brighton Run): however, this first rally was based at Clacton and, yes, Bedford coaches were there in force, dominating both the entry and the prize lists. During the summer the company announced a larger SB chassis with wheelbase increased to 5.486 metres (216 inches), accommodating 41 seater luxury coach bodies up to 9.144 metres (30 feet) maximum overall length, then in line with Ministry of Transport PSV regulations. Powered by the Bedford 4.9 litre petrol engine now developing 115 b.h.p. or the Perkins R6 108 b.h.p. diesel engine. The petrol engined version was priced at £855. Still in that same year, the first Bedford chassis was produced at the Dunstable factory on 2nd August, the move being part of the £36M expansion plan.

Another power unit had been announced in 1957, the Leyland 0.350 diesel, which had been introduced into the Bedford S series goods vehicle range, was made available for the SB chassis. This was short term for in 1958 Bedford's own 4.9 litre (300 cu.in) diesel was made available for the SB model.

During 1957 there was again the need for a small coach; Duple, realising this, mounted a 29 seater body – the re-introduction of the old Visa – on a modified 'C' type forward control chassis, in line with the P.S.V. legal regulations. A new Vista body with both 2.438 metres (96 inches) and 2.28 metres (90 inches) wide variants

Luxury coach bodywork by Strachen Spencer, again on SB chassis

Burlington coach/bus on SB chassis for Barton Motor Transport. (Right) VAS model 29/30 seat Duple 'Bella Vista'

was introduced. The narrow body was necessary for such locations as the Channel Islands, where 2.28 metres was the maximum legal vehicle width permitted.

After many years service the model OB faded out in the late 'fifties.

Vauxhall reviewed the P.S.V. market and decided to break away from the modified truck chassis with a specially designed 'V' range of Bedford chassis for bus and coach operation. In August 1961, the first range to be introduced was the VAS, a 29/30 seater. This was to be the smallest of the series with a wheelbase of 4.165 metres (164 inches) and to keep the low floor and step height 16 inch diameter wheel and tyre equipment was fitted. This was a return to the small bus and coach, which had earlier been abandoned. Two power units were available for the VAS, the Bedford 3.5 litre (214 cu.in) petrol engine and the 4.9 litre (300 cu.in) Bedford diesel engine.

A year later two more Bedford diesel engines were introduced; the 3.6 litre (220 cu.in) and 5.41 litre (330 cu.in): the latter replaced the 300 cu.in in the model SB chassis. With the 4.9 litre petrol and the Leyland 0.350 diesel, the operators were given the choice of three power units for the model SB.

Next came the VAL, a very unconventional chassis. The Ministry of Transport had introduced new legislation permitting 11 metre (36 feet) maximum overall length for P.S.Vs and there were various methods of taking advantage of the increase in overall length. Conventional, with 20 inch wheel and tyre equipment to accommodate the axle distribution loads, sacrificing the low floor height and requiring three steps or or even four for passenger entry. To keep the low floor line and minimum number of steps needed the continued adoption of the 16 inch wheel and tyre equipment, but while the rear twin tyre equipment of 16 inch diameter could accept the rear axle loading, the single front wheel and tyre equipment could not cope with the front axle loads. Bedford, after careful thought, decided to try to maintain the low floor height and two steps by fitting the smaller wheels and tyres, thereby adopting a twin steer configuration, 3 axles, two front and one rear. Whilst the scheme was unconventional for passenger transport it was not new; twin steer, 3 axles, had been operating on trucks for some years with success, while the twin front axle is also part of the goods transport eight wheelers.

The 'Cambrette' all metal bus body on a VAS chassis by Marshalls of Cambridge

A styled school bus by Anglo Coachbuilders of Batley on a VAS chassis
(Below) The Moseley Continental Sintra coach body by Caetano of Portugal on another VAS chassis

The chassis was designed for the mounting of a 55 seater body, the VAL, twin steer, 3 axles, could accommodate axle distribution and loading and the 11 metre maximum length overall body. The small wheels and tyres maintained the low floor height and centre of gravity and, combined with the long semi-elliptic leaf springs, gave the passengers a luxuriously smooth ride. The VAL had a wheelbase of 5.86 metres (231 inches) and was powered by the Leyland 0.400 six cylinder diesel engine, mounted at the front, drive being through a five speed gearbox with over-drive top gear; power steering and a very reasonable turning circle made the VAL a popular machine. The long front overhang allowed the front entrance to be ahead of the front wheels. With front mounted engines in public service vehicles there was always a restriction to passengers' entry through the front seats, caused by the engine cover protruding above the floor line. However, with careful body design the regulations governing the width of passageways were observed.

When first launched in 1961 the VAL P.S.V. chassis was priced at £1,775. The first body builder to design and mount bodies on the VAL chassis were Duple, with their 52 seater Vega Major, Plaxton, with their Embassy II for 52 seats, and the MCV, with their 49 seater all-metal Topaz. The Bedford 7.63 litre (466 cu.in) diesel engine was installed in the VAL chassis during the latter part of 1967 and was retained as the power unit until the end of the VAL production in 1972.

Three bodies on VAL chassis –
Duple 55 seater service bus
'Topaz' by Metropolitan Cammell
'Legionnaire' by Harrington

By Alexander of Falkirk for Highland Omnibus. There is a compartment for freight at the rear served by double opening doors and a single door on the nearside. (Right) VAM 45 seater with entrance ahead of the front wheels, the 'Pacesaver' by Strachens

1965 must be recorded as the year of two important events in the P.S.V. industry; the 50,000th Bedford passenger vehicle had been produced and selected for export to Australia, and Duple had produced their 25,000th body, which was mounted on a Bedford VAL chassis.

The third model of the 'V' series trio was the model VAM, introduced during the summer of 1965. Designed to accommodate from entrance bodies, the VAM provided a convenient seating layout inside, similar to that of the VAL. Even Duple seemed to have adopted the letter 'V' for their bodies with the offer of the Vista for the VAS chassis, the Viscount (introduced in 1966) for the VAM chassis and a 52 seater version of the Viceroy for the VAL chassis. Plaxton's name, Panorama, remained the same for all the three 'V' chassis.

The Commercial Vehicle Show in 1966 revealed a new Bedford diesel engine, the 7.63 litre (466 cu.in) six cylinder in-line, developing 145 b.h.p. At last, after

The Metropolitan, a 41/45 seater by Metro-Cammell Weyman, first launched in 1966 as the Athena.

a long wait, Bedford had designed and built a diesel engine suitable for all the truck, bus and coach chassis throughout the range, although it was not until the next year that it became available for the bus and coach chassis; then it became the standard power unit on the VAL and an optional unit to the 300 petrol engine on the VAM chassis.

Although British bus and coach dealers monopolised the Bedford chassis, however a Bedford coach dealer, Moseley, almost challenged the traditional British coach when he imported Portuguese built coaches mounted on Bedford chassis, built by Salvador Caetano of Oporto: the striking body of the Estorial, mounted on the VAL chassis, was followed by the Cascals on the VAM chassis and, twelve months later, by the 29 seater, the Sintra, on the VAS chassis.

Among service buses were to be found bodies by Strachens, the Pacemaker II, a 46 seater on the VAM chassis, followed by Alexander of Falkirk building a coach body with a freight compartment at the rear for Highland Omnibus on the VAM.

YRT long wheelbase chassis with Willowbrook body, the '007' Spacecar. Mid-engined

The 1970s started with more attention being paid to improved passenger entry and the high noise level from the front mounted engines. Vauxhall faced these problems and attempted to improve and overcome them. The first try was to tip the engine to improve the passageway in a similar manner to the Ford coach chassis, but they considered that this was not the final answer and eventually Vauxhall went for the principal of relocating the engine and power line amidships under the floor. From this they introduced the first Bedford underfloor amidships engined coach and bus chassis, designated the YRQ model. This was virtually the same as the model VAM chassis, but with the relocated engine. This configuration enabled a much improved passenger entry and the engine noise level in the saloon was lowered. This then made it a better proposition for the one-man, pay-as-you-enter bus application. The new model took the same power unit and mechanicals as the latest VAM model. Duple mounted their Viceroy up-to-date version and Plaxton their Elite on the YRQ. Later, Willowbrook of Loughborough offered their dual-purpose Expressway for bus service and luxury coach.

(Above, left) TRQ short wheelbase chassis with 'Panorama Elite II' by Plaxton (Above, right) 53 seat Duple Dominant on longer YRT

Duple 44 seat Viceroy body on YRQ, operated by Edinburgh City Transport

53 seater on YRT chassis by Marshall of Cambridge. Note the distinctive rake-back windscreen and high side windows

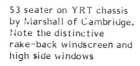

In 1972 the twin steer VAL chassis came under review and Vauxhall took a good look at the market; after all, the model had been in production and service successfully for ten years. Should they continue to market the VAL? If so, then the engine would have to be re-located amidships underfloor like the YRQ to satisfy entry and noise considerations.

Instead it was decided to replace the VAL with a new chassis ready for the big-coach market; designated the model YRT, the new replacement had a 5.638 metres (222 inch) wheelbase with the underfloor amidships power unit and drive, a 4 x 2 to accommodate a 53 seater body up to the full maximum overall length of 11 metres. It was powered by the new Bedford 7.63 litre (466 cu.in) diesel engine and was a heavy duty specification using axles as fitted on the 16 tonne KM truck series. The gross vehicle weight when introduced was 12,190 kgs (26,880 lbs). The bodies were for 53 seats; Duple with their all steel Dominant, Plaxton's Panorama Elite and the Willowbrook style that introduced the name '002'. The Moseley Continental offered the Caetono bodies Estorial II and, later in mid-1973, a service

The '002' Executive coach by Willowbrook on YRT chassis

Duple Dominant, a 53 seater on the 222 inch wheelbase YRT

Plaxton's Derwent service bus on 193 inch wheel- base YRQ

bus, the Camir was introduced by Marshalls of Cambridge. Later that year the short wheelbase YRQ was improved with an advanced braking system, power steering and better clutch operation, together with a high capacity gearbox. New model designations were allocated; the short wheelbase YRQ became the YLQ with a 138 b.h.p. version of the 500 range engines, and the long wheelbase YRT became the YMT, with the 157 b.h.p. version of the 500 range engines.

Show time once more: in 1976 the Vauxhall/Bedford stand exhibited the new midi-bus, model JJL. A thoroughly practical small/medium P.S.V. semi-integral chassis/body design. The power unit, the 5.41 litre (330 cu.in) diesel engine was mounted transversely at the rear of the body, driving through an automatic gearbox and equipped with with power steering as a standard requirement. With its 16 inch wheel and tyre equipment the JJL offered a low floor height. It had a wheelbase

Plaxton's bus on YMT chassis, 1979

of 3.4 metres (124 inches), overall length of 7.52 metres (296 inches) and a good turning circle of 15.24 metres (50 feet); it provided accommodation for 27 sitting and 10 standing passengers or, alternatively, 24 sitting and 11 standing, all ready for future seasons.

To be launched at the 1980 U.K. Motor Show at the National Exhibition Centre, held in October, was a new contender in the class of high powered 'long distance cruiser' coaches, the model YNT. Equipped with the 'Blue Series' 8.2 litre turbocharged diesel, this was the first Bedford coach chassis to top the 150kW (200 b.h.p.) power mark. The mid-ships engined 11 metre chassis was quiet and effortless to drive, with swift performances over long distances. Drive was through a Turner M6 six speed overdrive gearbox to a spiral bevel gear driven rear axle with a ratio of 5.31:1. The chassis incorporated all the features that had made Bedford the top choice of the independent operator, the quiet mid-mounted engine and drive line, outstanding ride and handling characteristics and economy of operation.

One of Bedford's features was low 'First cost' in relation to performance and power, plus well tried and proven components, a promise of high profit earning potential with the chassis. The 11 metre YMT continued in production alongside the 10 metre YMQ. Both had mid-engined chassis with the 8.2 litre 'Blue Series' turbo power featuring anti-roll bars front and rear and integral power steering. Transmission and rear axle revisions for the truck models also applied to Bedford bus and coach chassis.

In 1982 the Bedford design group at Vauxhall styled an aluminium 53 seater coach body for mounting on the YMT chassis to provide an outstanding combination of sleek looks, high strength, structural features, and an overall length of 12 metres (39 feet), now the new legal maximum overall length for P.S.Vs.

The YNY chassis frame had been extended to give a 6.1 metre (240 inch) wheelbase. The vehicle, called the 'Wright Contour' featured an inherently strong, yet light, body structure and priority had been given to safety factors and the easy repair of minor damage. Development was carried out in conjunction with Robert

Wright & Sons, Ltd., of Ballymena, County Antrim.

Initially, discussions between Bedford and Wright recognised the possibilities of the Alu-Suisse body structural system, which Wrights were licenced to produce. Thus the design department of Vauxhall had been allied with the established skills of a respected coachbuilder and the technologically advanced structural expertise of one of Europe's most substantial body engineering organisations. The body structure employed aluminium extrusions which were light in weight and very rigid, while the body components were grouped to permit fast, low cost repair or 'accident risk' areas. The Alu-Suisse system was also advanced in the application of modern materials; the rubber protection stripes along the body side, for example, also acted as hinges for the side lockers.

In researching the body concept Bedford Design undertook windtunnel testing on a one-eighth scale model at the Motor Industry Research Association (MIRA).

Aragon by Van Hool on YMT chassis

The object was to reconcile a striking trend-setting appearance with well researched aerodynamics characteristics. A further requirement to the body design was that it should minimise manufacturing and subsequent servicing costs. The front end appearance was distinguished by the use of a bonded one-piece raked windscreen and deep glass, with headlamps located behind the lower glass panel, badges etched on the lower glass and the absence of a large grille and other exterior protrusions. Surfaces at the rear of the body underwent changes during the windtunnel tests to establish the best shape to minimise drag and reduce dirt deposits.

The Alpha, a Portuguese-built Moseley Continental

High strength was a feature of the Alu-Suisse body structure, which had extended alloy planking to minimise the effects of side impact, while extruded pillars gave rigidity to resist the high forces associated with roll-over and other major impacts. Simple side skirt panels were readily replaceable in the event of damage. In the interior of the vehicle Bedford Design concentrated upon the entrance and the driver's area. Wright's approach to the saloon created an air of sophistication and elegant simplicity. There were 53 contoured Chardon reclining seats of French design, trimmed in grey/red moquette. Bedford Design had produced a neat, integrated appearance for the entrance area from the steps, leading to a functional and ergonomic driver's 'cockpit' and to instrumentation and storage facilities. Saloon comfort was further enhanced by a new system of ducted warm air heating fed in at low and high level and supplemented by an oil fired Eberspacher auxiliary unit, which could be programmed to pre-heat the saloon before departure.

The new coach was designed expressly for the 1983 Bedford YNT chassis, and featuring the mid-mounted 206 b.h.p. turbocharged Bedford 'Blue Series' diesel engine. Drive was through a ZF six speed gearbox, front and rear axle stabiliser bars were fitted.

The standard coach and bus models continued until the breakdown of the Bedford production in 1986.

1982. A coach for Luton Town Football Club and (below) a 53 seater based on the YNT chassis

Plaxton's Embassy, a 20 seat scaled-down version of their larger models

The 20 seat Moseley Continental Faro

A 17 seat coach by Plaxton, based on CF van chassis

20 seater Compact by Duple, based on J2 normal control truck chassis

12 seater Utilabus, a CF van conversion by Martin Walter

11 seater 'high-top' conversion of the CA light van by Martin Walter

ILLUSTRATIONS OF ODDITIES
AND EXPORT AND SPECIAL MODELS
OF TRUCKS

The following photographs show some of the special vehicles, oddities and models produced for both domestic and export markets –

Two Bedford chassis mounted back-to-back on train wheels for the Kowloon-Canton Railway

An S-type mounted on a rail bogey. Its engine had 3 carburettors and it spent many years hauling 50 ton loads of timber in a New Zealand lumber sidings with 1 in 10 gradients

Two overloads: a bus-truck in Cyprus and a heavily laden sawdust lorry, plus a trailer

B-type 12 cwt van converted for use as a heavy mower. (Below) V type 12 cwt van, 1935

An American advertising gimmick and a barrel on a WS 30 cwt chassis, 1934

A 10 seater vehicle on an early WLG 2 ton chassis in New Zealand
12 cwt V-type van of 1932/3

Lewin sweeper-collector. Side and three-quarter view in course of preparation and build

WH 2 tonner converted by Lewin as a sweeper-collector. Note the single rear wheels and the exposed steering column

TK removal van in Belgium

The 100,000th vehicle built: a TK

CF van and midi-bus in Germany
A radio control van – a special conversion – in Switzerland

TJ 2 ton normal control with box van body in Holland
TM 16 tonne box van in Italy

An O-type being used in oil exploration work in Tanganyika in 1954. (Below) TJ-type tractor unit, working in the forests of Malaysia. A modified 6 ton truck chassis

Royal Mail coach and van based on an early model, WLG 2 ton long wheelbase chassis. Mombasa-Malindi

WLG model, 2 ton long wheelbase, China

(Above) Two 3 ton TJ models. Normal control [Note absence of doors] Thailand
(Below) CA model vans in operation for Quebec National Gas Corporation

KM series. Locally built eight wheeler conversion in New Zealand. Also frequently met with in Australia

Fleet of 60 Bedford D series. 5 ton normal control. In Brazil: nearly 500 Bedford vehicles were shipped to Brazil in 1956.

ILLUSTRATIONS OF ODDITIES
AND EXPORT AND SPECIAL MODELS
OF BUSES AND COACHES

The following photographs show some of the special vehicles, oddities and models produced for both domestic and export markets –

100 passenger articulated bus built by Harringtons of Hove for BOAC, Hong Kong

Six wheeler conversion on the WLB bus chassis for Danish State Railways
Special touring bus, New Zealand. Rather small windows for observation by the passengers

A luxuious mobile caravan, sleeping six, on 1930 Bedford chassis. Included are kitchen, lounge, bedrooms, cocktail bar and other necessities

The 'Nightmare' grille with single centre headlamp. 1934 Bedford chassis and a Brazilian body builder

Pathan tribesmen in northern India seem to want to prove Bedford's 50% overload claim to be an understatement

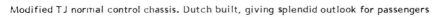

Modified TJ normal control chassis. Dutch built, giving splendid outlook for passengers

Three styles of grilles. Left, Portuguese on SB chassis; centre, Danish on modified truck chassis; right, American styled grille by a New Zealand body builder on SB chassis

27 seater on M model 4x4 chassis. Built for the Persian Gulf

OB chassis 26 seater by Louis Maes, Belgium
Another bus body by a Belgian body builder

36 seater coach built by Van Hool of Belgium, exhibited at the Brussels Show in 1950
An early R type 4 wheel drive chassis built for touring holidays in the tougher parts of Australia

POWER UNITS

When the first Bedford was announced in 1931 it was powered by the Vauxhall 3.177 litre six cylinder in-line petrol engine, developing 44 b.h.p. and given the R.A.C. rating of 26.33 h.p. for taxation purposes. The engine was based on the Chevrolet six cylinder unit used in the Chevrolet light trucks imported by General Motors. It was not long before the 3.177 litre engine was increased in power to develop 64 b.h.p by improving the carburation.

In 1938 the Bedford models demanded more power, consequently a new engine of 3.519 litres, six cylinder, in-line petrol, developing 72 b.h.p, and given an R.A.C. rating of 27.34 h.p. was released.

In the spring of 1950 another increase in engine power was required to maintain the Bedford truck range performance. This engine was basically the 3.519 litre six cylinder petrol, but with improved carburation to increase the power to 84 b.h.p; a lower power version of 76 b.h.p. was also released.

With Bedford's ever increasing gross weight models engine powers had to be increased accordingly, as in 1950, when a new petrol engine range was introduced for the 'S' series trucks. This new engine was 4.927 litres (300 cu.in) six cylinder in-line petrol developing 110 b.h.p; it was released for the 'S' series, with an increase in power to 115 b.h.p. at a later date.

The first diesel engine options that appeared were the Perkins diesel engines, the P6, R6 and P4.

Bedford began developing its own diesel engines, starting with a 300 cu.in (4.927 litres), which was a six cylinder, in-line, naturally aspirated, and developed 97 b.h.p.; then the 466 cu.in (7.63 litre) six cylinder, developing 145 b.h.p. Other diesel engines were developed and released for production such as 220 cu.in, 330 cu.in, 5.4 litre 'Red Series, 3.6 litre and the Blue Series 8.2 litre turbocharged. To supplement these diesels for heavier vehicles the Detroit Diesel range and the Cummins range were used.

There was a range of petrol engines over the years – 1.6 litre, 2.3 litre, 3.5 litre and 4.9 litre. Other smaller engines were used, developed for Vauxhall saloon cars and used in the lighter Bedford vehicles.

The last two ranges of diesel engines produced by Bedford before ceasing production were the 500 'Red Series' and the 8.2 litre 'Blue Series': to fully understand the depth of development going into these two diesel engine ranges a description is appended –

The new 8.2 litre 'Blue Series' diesels, announced on 29th February, 1980, resulted from the development of a 202 b.h.p. (151 kW) turbocharged engine, from which naturally aspirated variants arose, the first 'Blue Series' units to become generally available with inherently exceptional levels of ruggedness and durability.

These standards had been displayed by the 'Blue Series' it its proving trials. As most of the parts were identical with those of the turbocharged versions, the naturally aspirated 'Blue Series' engine had an unusually generous reserve of strength. It had a sleeved cylinder block, liberally ribbed for rigidity and quietness. An extra deep cylinder head permitted big water passages and accommodated large wide spaced valves with separate detachable valve guides and seat inserts. The exhaust valves were of high temperature distribution. The pistons were air-cooled. By using a deep cylinder head, room was provided, not only for larger water passages, but for a wider valve centre, which, in turn, caused the volumetric efficiency by affording bigger valves and freer port layout. A deep section head also gave rigidity and was able to distribute the clamping forces evenly over the gasket.

The most modern materials and valve gear technology went into the cylinder head design. The exhaust valves were forged from creep resistant nickel alloy, Nimonic 80, which was originally developed for gas turbines. Positive rotators were included in the exhaust valve and spring assembly, which turned the valves through an angle every time they opened, thus distributing the wear, evening out the heat flow between valve and seat and thus clearing off any deposits. Tappets and timing gears were turfrided to resist scuffing and to give long life.

Following long-standing Bedford practice the water flow was from end-to-end, flowing first along the cylinder block to the back, where it was then conducted into the rear of the cylinder head to flow down the length of the head to the front and out through the thermostat housing. This pattern of water flow eliminated water passages between block and head and through the gasket, the design of which was concentrated on gas and oil sealing. The gasket had a solid steel backbone, faced with a resilient composition and equipped with fire rings around the bores.

There was a streamlined flow of water through both block and head, preventing water from being entrained. As an aid to complete filling of the block a vent was located at the front of the cylinder block. With the cylinder head there was room for large quantities of water to circulate around the ports, valve seats and injectors. The injectors slid into tubes going right through the head's water jacket. These tubes were pressed into the bottom deck of the head and were sealed by 'O' rings at the top. The dual thermostat system was integral with the cylinder head. There was no waste of water flow through the by-pass when water was flowing through the radiator, which enabled a large by-pass pump to be used. As a result the flow of water around the engine increased when the thermostat shut off the flow through the radiator during warm-up or in cold weather.

Using this blocking by-pass arrangement much better cooling efficiency was obtained from a given radiator size. Having two thermostats enabled this increased water flow to be handled comfortably.

The cylinder head bolt incorporated a large diameter shoulder to distribute the load over the cylinder head casting and they were tightened by an intermittent torque process, which stabilises the friction in the threads and greatly reduced the likelihood of head bolt torque loss.

The cylinder block had a thick wall and incorporated many ribs which not only enhanced the rigidity and stabilised the bores, but also damped out a considerable amount of radiated noise. The Bedford engineers claimed that the 'Blue Series' was the quietest engine they had developed.

The design marked a return by Bedford to dry cylinder liners, which are of interference fit and flanged at the top. They were machined flush with the top of the cylinder block after fitting, so that the seal between cylinder block, gasket and head was kept as perfect as possible. Ultimately, in service, these liners could either be changed or could be bored out if necessary. The liners themselves were of high grade cast iron designed for resistance to wear and scuffing. They embodied a special honing pattern to help in retaining oil. The two-stage finishing process, called plateau-honing, increased the effective surface area to fight wear without spoiling the oil retention and gave good compatibility between pistons rings and bore.

Excellent temperature and scuffing resistance was achieved by fitting to each piston a top ring with a molybdenum inlay. There was a cast iron insert for the top groove. The second compression ring was of plain cast iron, taper-faced in order to speed up initial bedding. The back of the oil scraper ring was chromed, thus improving the life of the spring expander. A piston-cooling jet led up the centre of the connecting rod. To ensure plenty of bearing capacity the oil entry at the big end was angled so that it came outside the high pressure area of the bearing. Plenty of material surrounded the oiljet drilling, because the centre position of the shank of the 'H' section connecting rod was rectangle. The oil pump drive off the crank-shaft-nose was straddle-mounted, spreading the torque loads.

High rated variants of the naturally aspirated 8.2 litre 'Blue Series' range had a CAV in-line heavy duty Minipump fuel-injection pump. The lower rated engines had a CAV DPA rotary pump. Mechanical governors were used and the robust drive couplings on the in-line pumps were commonised with those used on the turbocharged engine.

The inlet porting was tangential to give vigorous rotary swirl to the air. Then, as the piston neared the top of its stroke, the squish effect on the air forced from the periphery of the piston and crown into the torodial combustion chamber or cavity superimposing a spiral swirl as well. This high air speed movement thoroughly mixed the fuel sprays from the injector, stopping the sprays from wetting the combustion chamber walls: smoother, efficient combustion resulted from this design.

The 'Blue Series' in turbocharged form developed 155 kW (208 b.h.p.) and, for the derated version, 154 kW (206 b.h.p.). The engine made a major contribution to Bedford's ability to match power and performance characteristics precisely to the needs of the operator in the key areas of heavy trucks and full-size coaches.

As the naturally aspirated 'Blue Series' engine inherited nearly all the basic engine features of the turbocharged parent, there were few differences between the two engines stripped of ancillary equipment, except for specific areas of reinforcement to give bigger strength margins to the high powered turbocharged unit. Included in this category are induction hardened crankshafts fillet radii (rather than rolled) to handle higher loadings. This piston, manufactured in low expansion aluminium alloy, was specifically designed for turbocharging and incorporated a wedge boss. The offset gudgeon pin gave optimum piston attitude in the bore and also of high strength. Externally, the turbocharged engine featured alternative Holset or Garrett Air Research, turbochargers with 'Ni-resist' cast iron turbine housings for hot strength. The three-piece exhaust manifold (designed for heat expansion tolerance) was the same 'Ni-resist' material, as were the sealing rings on the manifold joints. The turbocharger was centrally mounted on the left-hand side of the engine and clean air was drawn from the remotely mounted paper element air cleaner. The engine-mounted full-flow cooler obviated external piping and large cooling capacity gave extended oil life by controlling sump-oil temperatures to below 121°C (250°F).

The turbocharged Blue Series engine was equipped with the CAV HD Minipump six cylinder in-line fuel injection pump with a mechanical governor. It had a boost control device to reduce the amount of fuel delivered when the boost pressure was below a predetermined level to limit smoke during acceleration. Excess fuel was available to help cold starts and, when excess fuel was used, the pump was automatically retarded to obtain maximum cold-start timing. The turbocharged engine drove through a high-capacity 356 mm (14 inch) diameter dry plate clutch and the flywheel was fitted with a heavy duty bearing for the gearbox main drive pinion.

Installed power and torque ratings of the engine are –

TM trucks	power	155kW (208 b.h.p)
	torque	689 Nm (507 lbft)
YNT bus/coach	power	154 kW (206 b.h.p.)
	torque	684 Nm (503 lbft)

BS AU 141A

The comprehensive developments for the 1983 Bedford production were the extra-power Phase II variants of the 3.6 litre four cylinder and the 5.4 litre six cylinder 'Red Series' turbocharged diesel engines. The new 3.6 litre power unit output was lifted to 87 b.h.p. (64.9 kW) and replaced the existing unit of 72 b.h.p. (53.9 kW) turbocharged engine in the lighter truck variants. The new engine offered a 21% increase in power output over the turbocharged unit it replaced and a 34% increase over the equivalent naturally aspirated engine. The uprated 3.6 litre diesel engine developed 198 lbft (273 Nm) torque and became the standard for the 5½-7½ tonne TK/TL models.

Power output for the 5.4 litre six cylinder 'Red Series' turbocharged diesel engine rose to 135 b.h.p. (100.8 kW), as compared with 107 b.h.p. (79.9 kW) for the previous engine, a 26% increase or 38% up on the naturally aspirated equivalent. The 5.4 litre diesel engine developed 299 lbft (407 Nm) torque in its higher rated form. The Phase I 5.4 litre turbocharged, developing 107 b.h.p. (79.9 kW) was retained as a lower power option.

Many areas of design change for these extra power 'Red series' of Phase II, turbocharged version engines included –
* In-line fuel injection pump for the 5.4 litre only to meet fuelling requirements
* Increased boost for the 'tailored' turbocharger
* Strengthened main bearing cap bolts
* New Isoformic pistons with controlled expansion for closer tolerance and reduced noise
* Revised oil pump and drive, increase capacity on the 5.4 litre
* Twin-blocking by-pass thermostats for increased cooling efficiency, 5.4 litre only

The fuel injection equipment for the 5.4 litre diesel was a Bosch 'A' type in-line pump with RQV governor. This high-quality component was selected to give precise engine speed control and durability with increased output capacity. Fuelling for the 3.6 litre engine was by a Minimec 9mm in-line lift pump with a mechanical governor.

Combustion matched turbochargers by Holset and Garrett Air Research gave increased boost and, allied with tangential ports for maximum swirl, ensured efficient mixing of the fuel and air. Specific fuel economy of these new 'Red Series' variants was improved by up to 8% over the naturally aspirated equivalents. The

Phase II engines maintained the extended low-speed torque curves and engine flexibility that were an acclaimed feature of the naturally aspirated engines. The low-speed performance of the combustion system, for example, eliminated the need for a fuel pump boost-control which would otherwise reduce low-speed torque.

To accommodate higher crankshaft loads, the diameter of the main bearing cap bolts were increased to 15 mm. All crankshaft journals were induction hardened for extended durability. New, controlled-expansion 'Isoformic' pistons minimised tolerances for a closer fit and reduced noise. Fully machined torodial crown pistons and tangentially directed induction porting ensured optimum mixing of the fuel-air mixture for clean combustion. The cast iron top ring grooves inserts carried rings designed for maximum wear resistance. The top rings were barrel-faced with molybdenum inlays, while the second rings were taper-faced with internal steps. 150 psi oil rings gave optimum oil control.

The helical-gear driven oil pumps on the 5.4 litre diesel engine was revised for higher capacity at 59 litre/min.

The performance of the cooling system had been improved, high capacity twin-belt driven water pump being supplemented on the 5.4 litre engine by new, twin-blocking thermostats to give increased coolant flow. The high volume thermostat reduced warm-up time, while the thermo-sensing fan drive and low inertia GRP fan on the 5.4 litre engine minimised parasitic power losses. Bedford's unique end-to-end coolant-flow system provided maximum coolant circulation and gas-to-coolant blow-by, a major cause of head gasket failure in turbo engines, was eliminated.

Cylinder bolt heads in this range of engines gave maximum clamping load -a larger collar reduced under-head friction and bolt torque was increased by 19% for full gasket consumption. As for other Bedford engines, the cylinder head bolts were tightened by a special 'audited' torque process, preventing relaxation of the clamping loads.

From General Motor's Detroit Diesel Allison Division came the new 'Silver 92' series of diesel engines to power the heavier TM models. Introduced into the U.S.A. in 1981, these two-stroke six and eight cylinder diesel engines saw their first automotive application in Europe in these heavier TMs. The 'Silver 92' engines were advanced versions of the highly successful 92 series, combining all the proven benefits of these engines, with many new developments to increase efficiency and improve fuel consumption. All the 'Silver 92' diesel engines were turbocharged and aftercooled for extra power and greater economy.

Four versions of the 'Silver 92' series were available in the 1982 line up of the new TM tractors and rigids: one eight cylinder and three six cylinder engines.

Detroit Diesel 6V-92 TTA

The 'Torque-Tailored' turbocharged and aftercooled 6V-92 TTA was available to two power ratings of 236 b.h.p. (176 kW) and 266 b.h.p. (198 kW); both developed at 1950 r.p.m. as installed in the TM series. Torque ratings were 933 lbft (1267 Nm) at 1300 r.p.m. on both engines. The six cylinder vee configuration engine had a displacement of 9.05 litres. However, for the U.K. 236 b.h.p. could be specified in the new TM series, the TM3650 4 x 2 tractors, designed for operation at gross combination weights up to 36.5 tonnes. The higher powered 266 b.h.p. 'Silver 92' could be specified in the TM4400 model 4 x 2 tractors and the TM1900 4 x 2 rigids designed for operation at gross weights of 19 tonne and a gross train weight of up to 44 tonnes.

Detroit Diesel 6V–92 TA

This higher powered turbocharged and aftercooled engine developed 313 b.h.p. (233 kW) at 2100 r.p.m., with a torque rating of 1931 lbft (1264 Nm) at 1300 r.p.m. For use in the U.K. this unit was specified in the TM4400 tractor unit, providing a power to weight ratio of 9.6 b.h.p/tonnes when operating at the U.K. weight limit of 32.5 tonnes. The outfit was therefore well suited to long distance trucking operations where the emphasis was not only on economy, but on fast journey times.

Detroit Diesel 8V–92 TA

The highest rated 'Silver 92' engine was both turbocharged and aftercooled, developing a formidable output of 387 b.h.p (288 kW) at 1950 r.p.m. Torque rating was 1189 lbft (1615 Nm) at 1400 r.p.m. This powerful diesel engine was eminently suited to topweight heavy-duty haulage operations and long-haul Continental trucking at gross weights as high as 44 tonnes, but also requiring a high power to weight ratio of over 8 b.h.p./tonne.

The 'Silver 92' series incorporated many advanced features and improvements over the earlier 92 series to increase efficiency and improve consumption. The cylinder head was much stronger – the result of a breakthrough in foundry technique – and the head casting was completely redesigned. Camshaft and followers were polished to a microscopically smooth finish using the new Thielenhous honing process, resulting in more uniform lubrication, reducing friction and giving much longer life. To ensure optimum cooling major modifications were made to the water-pump to provide a more positive coolant flow resistance to cavitation at all engine speeds. Cylinder components had benefited from the new designs to increase their durability and efficiency. The turbocharger was matched to the air requirements of each individual model and its specific application to provide optimum combustion and high fuel efficiency. To increase the charge density of incoming air – which promotes improved fuel economy – the aftercooler had 33% more cooling fins to give a sizeable increase in air-to-water surface.

In addition to the specific improvements incorporated into the 'Silver 92' all the proven benefits of its predecessor were maintained, with power on every down-stroke for a quick, smooth response and lightweight vee configuration and compact overall dimensions.

The Cummins high performance diesel of 14 litre turbocharged type engines of the 'E' series had been proven in Bedford commercial vehicles, the TM series tractors and rigids, all of vertical six cylinder, in-line design. Three versions of the Cummins 'E' series were available in the 1980 production line-up of the TM tractors and six wheelers.

Cummins E255 turbocharged diesel

Developing 242.5 b.h.p. (181 kW) this was available as an optional power unit for the TM4400 32 ton GCW tractor.

Cummins E290 turbocharged diesel

Developing 277.4 b.h.p. (207 kW) this was available in the TM4400 32 ton GCW tractor unit, long wheelbase, also in the TM2600 6 x 4 (double drive sixwheeler) and the TM2600 6 x 2 (single drive sixwheeler) for both long and short wheelbases.

Cummins E370 turbocharged diesel

Developing 352 b.h.p. (262 kW) it was available as an optional power unit in the TM4400 32 ton GCW tractor.

Features of the Cummins 'E' series were thermostatically controlled oil cooling, high efficiency, multi pass air to water after cooling, 'Hi' lift cams and Molset M3b turbocharger. There were other premium engineering benefits, such as four valves per cylinder, pulse type exhaust manifolding to ensure peak long term operational efficiency, big cylinder displacement, generous bearing surfaces and hardened valve train. A large diameter camshaft controlling valve and injector movement manufactured from induction hardened alloy steel with gear drive was incorporated. Roller cam followers were used and the connecting rods were of the drop forged design, rifle drilled for pressure lubrication of the piston pins, which were taper ended to reduce unit pressure. There was a high tensiled strength steel forged crankshaft with induction hardened bearing journals and full counterweight. Alloy cast iron was used for the cylinder block and head. The cylinder block was fitted with removable wet liners. Each head served two cylinders, drilled for fuel supply and return lines, and corrosion resistant inserts were fitted in the exhaust valve seats. The fuel system was Cummins own design PT™ wear compensated system with integral flyball type governor and camshaft actuated DFF injectors.

TM3800 tractor unit, 4x2 powered by the Detroit-Diesel 8V-71 engine. 32 tons gross combination weight with sleeper cab, 1977

Index of Engine Specifications

Bedford 3.177 litre Petrol Engine
Bedford 3.519 litre Petrol Engine (RAC rating - 27.4 h.p.)
Bedford 3.519 litre Petrol Engine (RAC rating - 28 h.p.)

Model	3.177 litre (RAC rating - 26.33 h.p.		
No. of cylinders	6 in-line		
Bore			
Stroke			
Capacity (displacement)	3177 cc (193.8 cu.in.)		
Power	44bhp (32.8kW)	64bhp (47kW)	57bhp (42.5kW)
Torque			
Lubrication	Full pressurised system		
Fuel pump	Mechanical lift pump		
Carburettor			

Model	3.519 litre (RAC rating - 27.4 h.p.)		
No. of cylinders	6 in-line		
Bore	85.7mm (3.375 inches)		
Stroke	101.6mm (4 inches)		
Capacity (displacement)	3519 cc (214.7 cu.in.)		
Power	72bhp (53.7kW)	76bhp (56.7kW)	84bhp (62.6kW)
Torque	161 lbft (218Nm)	168.5 lbft (228Nm)	170 lbft (230.3Nm)
Lubrication	Full pressurised system		
Fuel pump	Mechanical lift pump		
Carburettor	Zenith 30V16-3	Zenith 30VIG7	Zenith 42 VIS-3

Bedford 300 cu.in Petrol Engine
Bedford 1.3 (45) Petrol Engine
Bedford 1.3 (25) Petrol Engine

Model	300	1.3 (45)	1.3 (25)
No. of cylinders	6 in-line	4 in-line	4 in-line
Bore	98.3mm (3.87in)	80.97mm (3.18in)	
Stroke	108mm (4.25in)	60.96mm (2.4in)	
Capacity (displacement)	4929cc (300cu.in)	1300cc (79cu.in)	
Power	115bhp (85.8kW)	42.5bhp (31.7kW)	24.1bhp (18kW)
Torque	2671 lbft (361.7Nm)	60.6 lbf (82.1Nm)	55.31 lbft (75Nm)
Lubrication	Full pressurised system		
Fuel pump	Mechanical lift pump		
Carburettor	Zenith 48 VIR	Zenith 3012E	Zenith 150CDSEU

Bedford 214 cu.in. Petrol Engine
Bedford 4.9 litre Petrol Engine

Model	4.92 litre	214 cu. in.
No. of cylinders	6 in-line	
Bore	98.4mm (3.87 ins)	85.7mm (3.375 ins)
Stroke	107.9mm (4.25 ins)	101.6mm (4 ins)
Capacity (displacement)	4927cc (300.5 cu.in)	3519cc (214.7 cu.in)
Power	113bhp (84.5kW)	80.5bhp (60kW9
Torque	223.5lbft (303Nm)	169lbft (229Nm)
Lubrication	Full pressurised system	
Fuel pump	Mechanical diaphragm lift pump	
Carburettor	37 VNR (DDL) Zenith	48 VIR Zenith

Bedford 1.6 litre Petrol Engine
Bedford 2.0 litre Diesel Engine
Bedford 1.6 litre Diesel Engine (GM)

Model	1.6 litre (P)	2.0 litre (D)	1.6 litre (D)
No. of cylinders	4 in-line		
Bore	82mm (3.2in)	86mm (3.4in)	80mm (3.14in)
Stroke	75mm (2.9in)	84mm (3.3in)	79.5mm (3.13in)
Capacity (displacement)	1584cc (96.6cu.in)	1951cc (119cu.in)	1598cc (97.5cu.in)

Power	79bhp (59kW)	46bhp (34kW)	53.6bhp (40kW)
Torque	85 lbft (116Nm)	73 lbft (98.5Nm)	70.8 lbft (96Nm)
Lubrication	Full pressurised system		
Fuel pump	Stromberg	N/A	N/A
Carburettor	Mechanical diaphragm lift pump		
Injection pump	N/A	Bosch VE	Bosch distributor
Injectors	N/A	Bosch	Bosch

Bedford 300 cu.in. Diesel Engine
Bedford 220 cu.in. Diesel Engine
Bedford 330 cu.in. Diesel Engine

Model	300 cu.in	220 cu.in	330 cu.in
No. of cylinders	6 in-line	4 in-line	6 in-line
Bore		103.2mm (4.063in)	103.2mm (4.063in)
Stroke		107.9mm (4.25in)	107.9mm (4.25in)
Capacity (displacement)	4917cc(300cu.in)	3614cc(220cu.in)	5420cc(330cu.in)
Power	97bhp (73.36kW)	65bhp (48.5kW)	98bhp (73kW)
Torque	200 lbft (271Nm)	148 lbft (201Nm)	227 lbft (309Nm)
Lubrication	Full pressurised system		
Fuel pump	Mechanical diaphragm lift pump		
Injection pump	Simms in-line		CAV-DPA
Injectors	-		

Bedford 466 cu. in. Diesel Engine

Model		466 diesel	
No. of cylinders		6 in-line	
Bore		115mm (4.562 in)	
Stroke		120mm (4.75 in)	
Capacity (displacement)		7.63 litre (466 cu.in.)	
Power	136bhp (101kW)	133bhp (99.4kW)	116bhp (86.7kW)
Torque			
Lubrication		Full pressurised system	
Fuel pump		Mechanical lift pump	
Injection pump		N/A	
Injectors		N/A	

Bedford 5.4/105TD Diesel Engine
Bedford 5.4/135TD Diesel Engine

Model	5.4 litre (5.4/105TD)	5.4 litre (5.4/135TD)
No. of cylinders	6 in-line	
Bore	103.2mm (4.06 in)	
Stroke	107.9mm (4.25 in)	
Capacity (displacement)	5407cc (330 cu.in.)	
Power	107.3bhp (80.1kW)	135.1bhp (100.8kW)
Torque	252lbft (343Nm)	300lbft (407Nm)
Lubrication	Full pressurised system	
Fuel pump	Mechanical lift pump	
Injection pump	CAV-DPA	Bosch in-line
Injectors	CAV 4 nozzle	

Bedford engines for the CF van and light truck range

Bedford 1.8/65 Petrol Engine
Bedford 2.3/80 Petrol Engine
Bedford 2.3/60 Diesel Engine

Model	1.8 litre	2.3 litre (P)	2.3 litre (D)
No. of cylinders		4 in-line	
Bore	85.73mm (3.375in)	97.54mm (3.84in)	92mm (3.622in)
Stroke	76.2mm (3 in)	76.2mm (3in)	85mm (3.346in)
Capacity (displacement)	1759cc (107cu.in)	2279cc (139cu.in)	2260cc (137.9cu.in)
Power	66bhp (49kW)	78bhp (58kW)	61bhp (45.5kW)
Torque	89lbft (120Nm)	124lbft (168Nm)	93.7lbft (127Nm)
Lubrication		Full pressurised system	
Fuel pump		Mechanical lift pump	
Carburettor	Zenith 361 VEP	Weber 341CT	N/A
Injection pump	N/A	N/A	Bosch in-line
Injectors	N/A	N/A	-

Bedford 8.2/130TD Diesel Engine (Blue Series)
Bedford 8.2/150 Diesel Engine (Blue Series)
Bedford 8.2/175TD Diesel Engine (Blue series)

Model	8.2 litre (130)	8.2 litre (150)	8.2 litre (175)
No. of cylinders		6 in-line	
Bore		115.9mm (4.625in)	
Stroke		129.5mm (5.1in)	
Capacity (displacement)		8198cc (500.3cu.in)	
Power	127bhp (95.1kW)	150.5bhp (112.2kW)	173.1bhp (129.2kW)
Torque	301 lbft (413Nm)	378 lbft (513Nm)	408.3 lbft (554Nm)
Lubrication		Full pressurised system	
Fuel pump		Mechanical lift pump	
Injection pump	CAV-DPA in-line	CAV heavy duty	CAV Minimec
Injectors		CAV 4 nozzle	
Turbocharger	Holset H2B	N/A	Holset H2B

View showing power unit. Location underfloor, mid-ships, also showing service access in the interior of the body. Models YNT and TRQ

Bedford 8.2/210TD Diesel Engine (Blue Series)
Detroit-Diesel 6V-92TTA Diesel Engine
Detroit-Diesel 6V-92TTA (265) Diesel Engine

Model	8.2 litre (210)	6V-92 TTA	6V-92 TTA
No. of cylinders	6 in-line	6 Vee formation	
Bore	115.9mm (4.62in)	123mm (4.842in)	
Stroke	129.5mm (5.1in)	127mm (5in)	
Capacity (displacement)	8198cc (500.3cu.in)	9054cc (552.3cu.in)	
Power	208.4bhp (155.5kW)	235.8bhp (176kW)	265.3bhp (198kW)
Torque	507.8lbft (689Nm)	933.8 lbft (1267Nm)	835 lbft (1133Nm)
Lubrication		Full pressurised system	
Fuel pump		Mechanical lift pump	
Injection pump	CAV or OMAP	Detroit Diesel - 9B90	
Injectors	5 hole nozzle	-	
Turbocharger	Holset H2B	Air Research TV 8102	

Detroit Diesel 6V-92 TA Diesel Engine
Detroit Diesel 6V-71 Diesel Engine
Detroit Diesel 8V-92 TTA Diesel Engine

Model	6V-92 TA	6V-71	8V-92 TTA
No. of cylinders	6 Vee formation		8 Vee formation
Bore	123mm (4.842in)	107.95mm (4.25in)	123mm (4.842in)
Stroke	127mm (5in)	127mm (5in)	127mm (5in)
Capacity (displacement)	9054cc (553.3cu.in)	6974cc (425.4cu.in)	12072cc (736cu.in.)
Power	312.2bhp (233kW)	221.1bhp (165kW)	385bhp (288kW)
Torque	931.6 lbft (1264Nm)	597.7 lbft (811Nm)	1190 lbft (1615 Nm)
Lubrication		Full pressurised system	
Fuel pump		Mechanical lift pump	
Injection pump	D.D. 9B90	D.D. N65	-

Cummins E255 Diesel Engine
Cummins E290 Diesel Engine
Cummins E370 Diesel Engine

Model	E255	E290	E370
No. of cylinders		6 Vee formation	
Bore		140mm (5.512in)	
Stroke		152mm (5.98in)	
Capacity (displacement)		14016cc (855cu.in)	
Power	242.5bhp (181kW)	277.4bhp (207kW)	351.1bhp (262kW)
Torque	835 lbft (1133Nm)	915.4 lbft (1242Nm)	1120.2 lbft (1520Nm)
Lubrication		Full pressurised system	
Fuel pump		Mechanical lift pump	
Injection pump		Pressure (PT)	
Injectors		Cummins 8 hole nozzle	

WHERE BEDFORDS WERE MADE

When Bedford commercial vehicles were first introduced by Vauxhall in 1931 they were built at the Luton plant. Output increased over the years with small expansions to the factory. By 1935 the annual production of all vehicles – cars and trucks – from the Luton plant topped the 50,000 mark from a workforce of some 8,000. Then came the Second World War and any further expansion was shelved.

With the War over and British industry struggling back to normal Vauxhall Motors took a long, hard look at its future. With the demand for both domestic and overseas markets the production capacity at Luton was inadequate, so the first major expansion was decided upon and actioned.

In 1948 work began on a new factory at Luton at the cost of £11 million and the 19½ acres site was soon a hive of industry and production. From the new plant the 7 ton 'S' series, forward control, Bedford trucks emerged, including a chassis for 39 seater bus or coach bodies. This expansion made more production space for the Vauxhall cars and production rose with the introduction of new car models. Over 12,000 people worked at the plant and production for 1952 reached 80,000 vehicles, but by the end of that year the Luton plant was becoming overcrowded and inadequate to produce both cars and trucks.

In 1953 the company's most ambitious building project was launched – £30 million was allocated to raise Vauxhall's production capacity to 250,000 units a year. To reach this production rate it was necessary to separate car and commercial vehicle production, so Dunstable, six miles away from Luton, was chosen as the site for a truck plant. By 1955 the new Dunstable factory was turning out Bedford vehicles.

The scope of the truck series widened still further with heavier models and Bedford petrol and diesel engines. The final stages of this costly expansion were completed in 1958 and, two years after the completion, the production target of 250,000 vehicles per year was achieved.

Further extensions were carried out to both the Luton and Dunstable factories and, with production well over the quarter million mark, home and export markets were increasing rapidly. Vauxhall Motors had to do something to meet the ever increasing demand and so ventured into the most expensive expansion in the company's history.

Because of Government policy it was not possible to expand further in either Luton or Dunstable; unemployment areas required vitalising to promote work, so Vauxhall decided on a site at Ellesmere Port in Cheshire, in the growing Merseyside Development Area. On a 395 acre site close to the River Mersey the new factory was built; the project, which was divided into three phases, cost a total of £68 million. The Ellesmere plant operated as a complete car factory, producing 170,000 vehicles a year with a workforce of almost 12,000. Apart from the complete manufacture of Vauxhall cars a number of mechanical units and components were supplied by the new plant for the Bedford plant at Dunstable.

Since Vauxhall Motors was a part of the American giant, General Motors

Corporation in Detroit, the British designers and engineers could take advantage of the vast test and research facilities of GMC in America. However, to obtain testing resources nearer home Vauxhall created its own research centre on a 58 acre site at Chaul End; the facilities included various laboratories, including the first radioisotope laboratory within the British motor industry. To provide further facilities Vauxhall procured a 700 acre site at Millbrook, 18 miles from the Luton plant, for a splendid proving ground, which was completed in 1971, a part of the Engineering Department's very comprehensive facilities for vehicle development and testing. The proving ground has a two mile five-lane high speed banked circular track, a 3.3 mile hill circuit, a mile long four-lane straight and level track and a one mile cross country course. Also available was the dust tunnel, water splash, steering test pad, a 75 ton concrete impact barrier and an impact simulator in the safety laboratory, which, with other units, together gave Vauxhall a proving ground as fine as any in Europe.

Towards the end of 1964 a new £2¼ million Engineering & Styling Centre came into use at Luton, housing, under one roof, most of the staff engaged in the design and development of new Vauxhall cars and Bedford commercials. Basically, it was divided into two sections, engineering drawing offices and workshops and styling design studios and styling workshops.

When a new Bedford series was proposed the first move was with the product planners who, having investigated the market, advised engineering on various aspects of consumer demand. The draughtsmen and development engineers would get together to produce layouts of the proposed vehicle, then detailed drawings followed, to be translated into sheet metal panels, engines, gearboxes, axles, etc. Meanwhile the styling engineers were producing designs and clay models of the truck cab; prototypes built received exhaustive testing at Millbrook proving ground and frequently in far distant parts of the world where extremes of temperature and surface conditions might be encountered. Finally, at the end of a very long, complex and costly period of development, testing and refining, a newly designed Bedford truck chassis was passed to production.

The watchdogs standing over dimensional accuracy in the production areas were the staff of the Quality Control Centre; a new Centre had come into operation for both Luton and Dunstable plants in 1965. These quality control specialists were responsible for the accuracy of the tools, jigs and fixtures and equipment used to produce component parts and assemblies, together with all bought out finished part, going to make the Bedford truck chassis.

The work of the Quality Control was far reaching, starting with the arrival of the first component for assembly. Samples, whether from outside sources or from within the plants, had to conform to specifications, including metallurgical and chemical acceptance. The checks covered a variety of materials from plastics to paint; from felt to forgings; from carpets to castings. The responsibility was to ensure that materials were processed, finished, assembled and functioned in the way laid down by design requirements. Quality control was carried out at all stages of manufacture. Additionally, vehicles were selected, at random, from the line to be subjected to a series of checks and road testing by a team of 'auditors' working for the Reliability Department, the purpose being to ensure that quality control standards are correct and conform with those of the customer. Both departments were aware that the project would eventually be subjected to its greatest test and critical inspection of all – that of the customer.

Production began in the press shop, covering a quarter of the 1½ million square feet of the car production building. Here steel arrived in huge 15 ton coils or in baled sheets. The steel was shaped in the press shop into panels and other steel parts to make the Bedford truck cabs. Painting, too, was a highly complex process: paint is more than giving good looks, it must protect the metal cab, inside and outside, as well as underneath. The first stage in painting was a seven part rust proofing process, followed by a total immersion in a 500 gallon tank of paint, which was then baked on. Then the entire cab underbody received a thick coat of tough bituminous compound and, finally, four full coats of the finishing colour in high lustre, hard wearing acrylic paint. From paint to trim, through many stations where different items were fitted, from floor covering carpets, to seats, to door handles and to window glass.

Finally, down the assembly line the bare chassis frame received front and rear axles, springs, brake systems, fuel tank and pipes, engine and gearbox assembly, drive line, wheels and tyres, the cab and other items. With all the smaller components fitted, the Bedford truck chassis rolled of the assembly line ready for work.

A milk delivery conversion of a 1933 12 h.p. ASYC model

Four wheel drive military R-type in civilian garb, helping to build the M1 motorway

MODEL DESIGNATIONS

'Astra'	7.5 cwt light van
ASXC	8 cwt van (14 h.p.)
ASYC	8 cwt van (12 h.p.)
BXC	12 cwt van (3.177 L)
BYC	12 cwt van (17 h.p.)
C	4 tons to 6 tons forward control trucks
CAL	10/12 cwt long wheelbase
CAS	10/12 cwt short wheelbase
CF230	1.06 ton van/truck
CF250	1.25 ton van/truck
CF280	1.36 ton van/truck
CF350	1.95 ton van/truck
CF350L	2.22 ton chassis cab
D	25 cwt to 3 tons
D	4 tons to 6 tons and 8 ton tractor unit
HA110	0.35 ton light van
HA130	0.52 ton light van
HC	5/6 cwt van
JC	10/12 cwt van
K	30 cwt
KB26	1.21 ton pick-up (P)
KB41	1.12 ton pick-up 4 x 4 (P)
KBD26	1.12 ton pick-up (D)
KBD41	1.04 ton pick-up 4 x 4 (D)
MLD	2/3 ton long wheelbase
MSD	2/3 ton short wheelbase
OLA	3/4 ton long wheelbase
OLB	5 ton long wheelbase
OSA	3/4 ton short wheelbase
OSB	5 ton short wheelbase
OSS	8 ton tractor unit
PC	Re-designated JC
R	3 ton 4 x 4 (S series)
S	7 ton short wheelbase
S	7 ton long wheelbase
S	10 ton tractor unit
TA2	2 ton short wheelbase
TA2P	Pick-up truck
TA3	3 ton short wheelbase
TA3	3 ton long wheelbase
TA4	4 ton short wheelbase
TA4	4 ton long wheelbase
TA5	5 ton short wheelbase
TA5	5 ton long wheelbase

WTB 26 seater, 1935

The dashboard of the YRQ

Service buses by Mulliner operated by Walsall Corporation

TASS	8 ton tractor unit
TJ	25 cwt to 7 tons and 8 ton tractor unit
TK570	3.45 ton truck range
TK750	4.95 ton truck range
TK860	4.63 ton truck range
TK1000	6.82 ton truck range
TK1260	9.11 ton truck range
TL570	3.2 ton truck range
TL750	4.9 ton truck range
TL860	5.5 ton truck range
TL1000	6.8 ton truck range
TL1020	6.6 ton truck range
TL1260	9.09 ton truck range
TL1500	10.44 ton truck range
TL1630	11.32 ton truck range
TL1630	16 ton GCW tractor
TL1930	19 ton GCW tractor
TM1700	11.62 ton truck range
TM1900	10.6 ton truck series
TM2500	24.6 ton GCW tractor
TM2600	19.3 ton truck 6 x 2
TM2600	19.1 ton truck 6 x 4
TM3250	32 ton GCW tractor
TM3650	32 ton GCW tractor
TM4400	32 ton GCW tractor
VXC	12 cwt van (3.177 l)
VYC	12 cwt van (16.9 h.p.)
WHG	2 ton short wheelbase
WLG	2 ton long wheelbase
WS	30 cwt
WTH	3 ton short wheelbase
WTL	3 ton long wheelbase

Notes:

(D) diesel model series
(P) petrol model series
GCW gross combination weight (for
articulated vehicles)

12 h.p. 8 cwt van,
model ASYC, 1933

Appendix 2

SPECIFICATIONS

TRUCK – 'W' SERIES

The 'W' series was the first commercial vehicle range Vauxhall achieved under the Bedford marque.
Long and short wheelbases for the 2 ton version, models WHG and WLG.
Short wheelbase only for the 30 cwt version, model WS.
Later the 'W' series was joined by by 3 ton, with both short and long wheelbases: they differed to the 30 cwt and 2 ton with a short bonnet, models WTH and WTL.
Powered by the 3.177 litre six cylinder Bedford petrol engine.
Drive line included a four speed crash change gearbox with the following ratios –
1st 7.22:1; 2nd 3.47:1; 3rd 1.71:1; 4th 1.0:1; reverse 7.1:1

Models	WHG	WLG	WS	WTH
Type		2 ton	30 cwt	3 ton
Wheelbase	3.32m (131in)	3.98m (157in)	3.32m (131in)	2.79m (111in)
GVW				
Kerb weight				
Payload (approx)	2032kg (4480 lb)	2032kg (4480 lb)	1524kg (3360 lb)	3047kg (6720 lb)
Engine		3.177 litre six cylinder petrol		
Gearbox		Four speed crash change		
Rear axle ratio		4.714:1		
Front suspension		Semi-elliptic longitudinal leaf springs		
Rear suspension		Semi-elliptic longitudinal leaf springs		
Brakes				
System		Mechanically operated		
Front diameter				
Front width				
Rear diameter				
Rear width				
Wheels	3.75 x 20		4.33 x 20	
Tyres				
Front		32 x 6 TT		
Rear				
Fuel tank capacity				
Electrical				
System		6 volt Lucas generator		
Battery		6 volt 100 amp/hour		
Turning circle				

Notes: Model WTL had identical specifications as WTH, except wheelbase of 3.98m (157 in).
Later the wheelbase was reduced. The short wheelbase WHG became 3.04 metres (120 inches) and the long became 3.632 metres (143 inches)

TRUCK – VYC and VXC series

A normal control van of 12 cwt payload capacity. Using the Vauxhall 16.9 h.p. 'Cadet' six cylinder engine and mechanicals. The original version of 1932, model VYC, was equipped with disc wheels which were, in 1934, changed to wire wheel design. The VXC differs by the installation of a larger petrol engine, the Bedford 3.177 litre six cylinder, as used in the 30 cwt and 2 ton models.

Models	VYC	VXC
Type	12 cwt van	
Wheelbase	2.69m (106in)	
GVW		
Kerb weight		
Payload (approx)	609kg (1344lb)	
Engine	16.9 h.p.petrol	3.177 litre petrol
Gearbox	3 speed	
Rear axle ratio		
Front suspension	Semi-elliptic longitudinal leaf springs	
Rear suspension	Semi-elliptic longitudinal leaf springs	
Brakes		
System	Mechanically operated	
Front diameter		
Front width		
Rear diameter		
Rear width		
Wheels	Wire spoke	
Tyres		
Front		
Rear		
Fuel tank capacity		
Electrical		
System	6 volt Lucas generator	
Battery	6 volt	
Turning circle		

Notes: The 16.9 h.p. six cylinder petrol engine is the same as that used in the Vauxhall 1932 'Cadet' saloon car.
The 3.177 litre six cylinder petrol engine is the Bedford 26.33 h.p. truck engine.

TRUCKS – K, M and O series

The K, M and O series brought a complete range of trucks to the operator. Based on identical design, covered payloads from 30 cwt to 5 tons, including a 6/8 ton articulated tractor unit.
Designated model identification, as follows

    K   30 cwt with the KV a van model. One wheelbase

M	MSD short wheelbase 2/3 ton, and		
	MLD long wheelbase 2/3 ton		
O	OSA short wheelbase 3/4 ton,		
	OLA long wheelbase 3/4 ton,		
	OSB short wheelbase 5 ton,		
	OLB long wheelbase 5 ton,		
	OSS short wheelbase only, 6/8 ton articulated tractor unit, and		
	OB special long wheelbase suitable for 26/32 seater bus or coach		

Powered by a 3.519 litre six cylinder petrol engine.

Drive line included a four speed crash change gearbox with the ratios – 1st 7.22:1; 2nd 3.47:1; 3rd 1.71:1; 4th 1.0:1; reverse 7.15:1

Models	K	M	O
Type	30/40 cwt	2/3 ton	3/4 ton
Wheelbase	3.048m (120in)	3.048m (120in)	2.819m (111in)
GVW	4063kg (8960 lb)	5587kg (12320 lb)	7619kg (16800 lb)
Kerb weight	1777.7kg (3920 lb)	1981kg (4370 lb)	2471kg (5450 lb)
Payload (approx)	1524kg (3360 lb)	2031kg (4480 lb)	3047kg (6720 lb)
	2031kg (4480 lb)	3047kg (6720 lb)	4063kg (8960 lb)
Engine	3.519 litre six cylinder petrol		
Gearbox	Four speed crash change		
Rear axle ratio	4.714:1		5.86:1
Front suspension	Semi-elliptic longitudinal leaf springs		
Rear suspension	Semi-elliptic longitudinal leaf springs		
Brakes			
System	Hydraulic operated. Vacuum assistance, except K		
Front diameter	330.2mm (13in)		355.6mm (14in)
Front width	N/A		
Rear diameter	355.6mm (14in)		
Rear width	N/A		
Wheels	4.33 x 20	3.75 x 20	4.33 x 20 (3 ton)
Tyres			5.00 x 20 (4 ton)
Front	32 x 6		32 x 6 HD (3 ton)
			34 x 7 HD (4 ton)
Rear	32 x 6 HD	32 x 6 TT	32 x 6 HD (3 ton)
			34 x 7 HD (4 ton)
Fuel tank capacity			
Electrical			
System	6 volt Lucas generator C39		
Battery	6 volt 100 amp/hour		
Turning circle	13.1m (43ft)		11.9m (39ft)

Variants

K series one wheelbase only, as shown in specification

M series short wheelbase of 3.048m (120in) as shown in specification and long wheelbase of of 3.63m (143in)

O series short wheelbase 2.819m (111in) as shown in specification and long wheelbase of 3.98m (157in)

Models	OSB	OLB	OSS
Type		5 ton	8 ton tractor
Wheelbase	2.819m (111in)	3.98m (157in)	2.819m (111in)
GVW		8838.1kg (19488 lb)	12190kg (26880 lb)
Kerb weight	2539kg (5600 lb)	2734kg (6030 lb)	N/A
Payload (approx)	5079kg (11200 lb)	5079kg (11200 lb)	8127kg (17920 lb)
Engine		3.519 litre	
Gearbox		Four speed crash change	
Rear axle ratio		5.86:1	7.4:1
Front suspension		Semi-elliptic longitudinal leaf springs	
Rear suspension		Semi-elliptic longitudinal leaf springs	
Brakes			
System		Hydraulically operated. Vacuum servo assisted	
Front diameter		355.6mm (14in)	
Front width		N/A	
Rear diameter		355.6mm (14in)	
Rear width		N/A	
Wheels		5.00 x 20	4.33 x 20
Tyres		34 x 7 HD	32 x 6 HD
Front		8.25 x 20	32 x 6 HD
Rear		N/A	
Fuel tank capacity			
Electrical			
System		6 volt generator	
Battery		6 volt 100 amp/hour	
Turning circle	12.8m (42ft)	17.98m (59ft)	11.88m (39ft)

TRUCK – CA series van

The CA series, Bedford's semi-forward control van models covered 10/12 cwt and 15 cwt for both short and long wheelbases. Gross vehicle weights of 1678kg (3700lb) to 1905kg (4200lb) earned an enviable reputation for toughness and the ability to take whatever the task. A great favourite among the newspaper delivery agents and local traders.

Models	CAS		CAL	
Type	10/12 cwt	15 cwt	10/12 cwt	15 cwt
Wheelbase		2.286m (90in)		2.591m (102in)
GVW	1678kg (3700 lb)	1859kg (4100 lb)	1723kg (3800 lb)	1905kg (4200 lb)
Kerb weight	969kg (2136 lb)	988kg (2178 lb)	1014kg (2236 lb)	1033kg (2278 lb)
Payload (approx)	508kg (1120 lb) 609kg (1344 lb)	762kg (1680 lb)	508kg (1120 lb) 609kg (1344 lb)	762kg (1680 lb)
Engine		1.507 litre petrol. 4 cylinder		
Gearbox		3 speed synchromesh		
Rear axle ratio		5.285:1		
Front suspension		Independent wishbone & coil spring		
Rear suspension		Semi-elliptic longitudinal leaf springs		

Brakes	CAS	CAL
System	Hydraulically operated	
Front diameter	232mm (9.13in)	
Front width	N/A	
Rear diameter	232mm (9.13in)	
Rear width	N/A	
Wheels	Disc	
Tyres		
Front	5.90 x 15. 6 ply 6.40 x 15. 6 ply	5.90 x 15. 6 ply 6.40 x 15. 6 ply
Rear	As Front	
Fuel tank capacity	N/A	
Electrical		
System	12 volt generator (257 watt)	
Battery	12 volt	
Turning circle	10.36m (34ft)	11.27m (37 ft)

TRUCK – 'S' series. Forward control

Bedford's first factory produced civilian forward control series. 7 ton payload covering haulage work with the short and long wheelbase versions and tipper work with the short wheelbase version. Included in the series was a 10 ton payload articulated tractor unit. A new petrol engine of 300 cu.in. capacity, six cylinder in-line, was designed for the series. A great favourite with hauliers and construction work on site.

Four speed synchromesh gearbox with the ratios - 1st, 7.059:1; 2nd, 3.332:1; 3rd, 1.711:1; 4th 1.0:1. Five speed synchromesh gearbox offered as optional equipment with ratios - 1st, 6.93:1; 2nd, 3.78:1; 3rd, 2.24:1; 4th, 1.47:1; 5th 1.0:1

Type	7 ton	7 ton	10 ton tractor
Wheelbase	2.94m (116in)	3.96m (156in)	2.18m (86in)
GVW			
Kerb weight			
Payload (approx)	7111kg (15680 lb)	7111kg (15680 lb)	10158kg (22400 lb)
Engine	300 cu.in. 6 cylinder petrol		
Gearbox	4 speed synchromesh		
Rear axle ratio	Ratios available 5.83:, 6.8:1 & 5.3:1		
Front suspension	Semi-elliptic longitudinal leaf springs		
Rear suspension	Semi-elliptic longitudinal leaf springs		
Brakes			
System	Hydraulically operated vacuum servo assisted		
Front diameter	N/A		
Front width	N/A		
Rear diameter	N/A		
Rear width	N/A		
Wheels	B6.0 x 20		
Tyres	8.25 x 20. 12 ply		
Fuel tank capacity	118 litres (26 gallons)		

Electrical
  System   12 volt generator
  Battery   2 x 6 volt 120 amp/hour
Turning circle   N/A

TRUCK – TA series

Normal control truck series with payloads from model TA2 at 2 tons to model TA5 at 5 tons. Powered by the 3.519 litre six cylinder petrol engine and the four speed synchromesh gearbox with the ratios – 1st, 7.06:1; 2nd, 3.33:1; 3rd, 1.71:1, 4th, 1.0:1.
Perkins P6 six cylinder diesel engine as optional on model TA4 at 4 tons and model TA5 at 5 tons.

Models	TA2	TA3	TA4	TA5
Type	2 ton	3 ton	4 ton	5 ton
Wheelbase	3.02m (119in)		3.04m (120in)	4.24m (167in)
GVW	3178kg (7000 lb)	5339kg (11760lb)	6864kg (15120lb)	8163kg (18000lb)
Kerb weight	1564kg (3445 lb)	1818kg (4005 lb)	2070kg (4560 lb)	2378kg (5245lb)
Payload (approx)	1614kg (3559 lb)	3521kg (7764 lb)	4794kg (10570lb)	5079kg (11200lb)
Engine	4.728 litre six cylinder petrol			
Gearbox	4 speed synchromesh			
Rear axle ratio	4.7:1	5.28:1	5.83:1	7.4:1
Front suspension	Semi-elliptic leaf springs			
Rear suspension	Semi-elliptic leaf springs			
Brakes				
System	Hydraulic operated. Vacuum assisted, except model TA2			
Front diameter	330.2mm (13in)		355.6mm (14in)	
Front width	44.4mm (1.75in)		53.8mm (2.12in)	107.9mm (4.25in)
Rear diameter	330.2mm (13in)		355.6mm (14in)	
Rear width	44.4mm (1.75in)	82.5mm (3.25in)	53.8mm (2.12in)	107.9mm (4.25in)
Wheels			N/A	
Tyres	7.50 x 16. 8 ply	6.50 x 20. 8 ply	7.00 x 20 10 ply	7.50 x 20 10ply
Fuel tank capacity		N/A		
Electrical				
System		N/A		
Battery		N/A		
Turning circle		N/A		

TRUCKS – 'HA' series

The model 'HA' series was a thoroughly proven van range for payloads from 7 cwt (the HA110) to 10 cwt (the HA130). Normal control types giving passenger car comfort. Good loading space and wide opening rear doors. The floor was covered with rot proofed wood, easy on the cargo, easily replaced and kept clean. The front grille was flat, incorporating combined side and head lamps and also front flashers. Two power units available, both four cylinder petrol engines of 42.5 b.h.p and an economy version developing 24.1 b.h.p. Four speed gearbox synchromesh on all forward gears. Single speed rear axle with two rated capacities, 710kg (1565 lb) for the model HA110 and 890kg (1963 lb) for the model HA130. Dual circuit braking system, with independent circuits for front and rear hydraulically operated wheel brake assemblies. Offered with the usual passenger car electrics and equipment. All steel welded constructed chassis frame and body, integral panel van with two hinged cab doors and double rear hinged doors. Gearbox ratios – 1st, 3.76:1; 2nd, 2.213:1; 3rd, 1.404:1; 4th, 1.0:1; reverse 3.707:1

Models	HA110		HA130
Type	92170	92170C088	923370
Wheelbase		2.32m (90in)	
GVW		1120kg (2469 lb)	
Kerb weight		764kg (1684 lb)	789kg (1739 lb)
Payload (approx)		356kg (785 lb)	531kg (1171 lb)
Engine	1.3 litre (45)	1.3 litre (25)	1.3 litre (45)
Gearbox		4 speed (floor mounted gearshaft)	
Rear axle ratio	4.125:1	3.888:1	4.125:1
Front suspension		Independent wishbone arms, single transverse spring	
Rear suspension		Semi-elliptic leaf springs (6 leaves)	
Brakes			
System		Hydraulically operated	
Front diameter		203mm (8in)	
Front width		44.5mm (1.75in)	
Rear diameter		203mm (8in)	
Rear width		38.1mm (1.5in)	
Wheels		4J x 12	
Tyres	5.50 x 12C	155 SR 12	155 SR x 12 tubed
Fuel tank capacity		33 litre (7 gallon)	
Electrical			
System		12V 45A alternator	
Battery		12V 40 amp/Hour	
Turning circle		10.5m (34ft 5in)	

TRUCKS – 'Astra' van series

Based upon one of Europe's top selling cars, the 'Astra', during the 80's, set a new standard in comfort, styling and economy, combined with a practical load capacity. Payload of 381kg (7.5 cwt). Two power units were offered, the 1.3 litre four cylinder petrol engine, developing 73.7 b.h.p., and the GMC 1.6 litre diesel engine, developing 53.6 b.h.p. Four speed gearbox synchromesh on all forward gears, with the option of an automatic transmission, the GMC CM40. Diagonally split, dual circuit hydraulically operated brakes with servo assistance. Front discs and rear drum types. Offered with the usual passenger car electrics and equipment. All steel welded construction chassis frame and body, integral panel van with two hinged cab doors and tailgate type rear door. Towing eyes front and rear.

Gearbox ratios

4 speed manual. 1st, 3.636:1: 2nd 2.211:1; 3rd, 1.429:1; 4th 1.0:1; reverse, 3.182:1. For 1.3 litre petrol engined versions

1st, 3.545:1, 2nd, 2.158:1; 3rd, 1.37:1; 4th, 0.971:1; reverse, 3.333:1. For the 1.6 litre diesel engined version

GMC.CM40 3 speed – P-Park. N-Neutral. D-2.84:1, 1.601:1 1.0:1. 2-2.841:1, 1.6:1. 1-2.84:1

Type	9TD70	9TD70 (C.L53)
Wheelbase	2.52m (99 in)	
GVW	1420kg (3131 lb)	1530kg (3374 lb)
Kerb weight	895kg (1973 lb)	985kg (2172 lb)
Payload (approx)	525kg (1157 lb)	545kg (1202 lb)
Engine	1.3 litre petrol	1.6 litre diesel
Gearbox	4 speed manual	
Rear axle ratio	4.18:1	3.74:1
Front suspension	Independent with McPherson struts & coil springs	
Rear suspension	Compound crank, miniblock coil springs	
Brakes		
System	Hydraulically operated with servo assistance	
Front diameter	236mm (9.3in) discs	
Front width	43.9mm (1.73in)	
Rear diameter	200mm (7.87in) drums	
Rear width	45mm (1.77in)	
Wheels	5J x 13	
Tyres	155 SR 13 radials	
Fuel tank capacity	50 litres (11 gallons)	
Electrical		
System	12V 45A alternator	
Battery	12v 44 amp.hour	12V 66 amp/hour
Turning circle	10.45m (34ft 3in)	

The Astra series has 4 versions, differing by the type of power unit, gearbox, rear axle ratio and the battery capacity.

Type 9TD70 (C,M40) differs only in the transmission, installation of the 3 speed automatic, from the standard type

9TD70.

Type 9TD70 (C.L53,M40) differs in the transmission, the installation of the 3 speed automatic, from the standard diesel model type 9TD70 (C.L53).

TRUCKS - 'CF' van and light truck series

The 'CF' series covered both vans and light trucks, varying from gross vehicle weights of 2340kg (5160 lb) to 3500kg (7717.5 lb). The CF230 and CF250 with gross vehicle weights of 2340kg and 2570kg (5666 lb) earned an enviable reputation for toughness and ability to take whatever the task. The smaller pair had a wheelbase of 2.69m (106in), giving a load capacity of 208 cu. ft., available as vans, chassis cabs for light truck bodies and other special bodies, and the chassis cowls for special bodies.

The larger versions, the CF280 and CF350 vans and light trucks varied from 2830kg (6240 lb) GVW for the CF280 and 3500kg for the CF350. Wheelbases of 3.2m (126in) give a load capacity of 270 cu. ft.

All versions were available with optional power units:

CF230 - standard 1.8 litre four cylinder petrol; optional 2.3 litre four cylinder diesel.

CF250, CF280, CF350 - standard 2.3 litre four cylinder petrol; optional 2.3 litre four cylinder diesel.

Two gearboxes provided - the Bedford 4 speed synchromesh for CF230 and CF250 and the ZF 4 speed synchromesh for CF280 and CF350.

An extra long wheelbase of 3.556m (140in) for model CF350L chassis cab and chassis cowl, with similar specification to the CF350 standard model.

Van was an all steel welded integral construction with inverted top-hat section under floor reinforcement. For chassis cowl and chassis cab versions double top-hat section ladder type chassis frame from the rear of the cab, with mild steel longitudinal and crossmembers sections. Welded construction throughout. With passenger car electrical equipment, comfort and trimmings.

Models	CF230	CF280
Type	97170	97570
Wheelbase	2.69m(106in)	3.2m (126in)
GVW	2340kg (5159.7 lb)	2830kg (6240 lb)
Kerb weight	1396kg (3078 lb)	1529kg (3371 lb)
Payload (approx)	944kg (2081 lb)	1301kg (2869 lb)
Engine	1.8 litre petrol	2.3 litre petrol
Gearbox	Bedford 4 speed synchromesh	ZF 4 speed synchromesh
Rear axle ratio	4.63:1	5.22:1
Front suspension	Independent upper & lower suspension arms. Coil springs	
Rear suspension	Semi-elliptic leaf springs - single taper or multi leaf	
Brakes		
System	Hydraulically operated. Independent circuits front/rear	
Front diameter	229mm (9in)	254mm (10in)
Front width	69.9mm (2.75in)	

Rear diameter	229mm (9in)	254mm (10in)
Rear width	44.5mm (1.75in)	57.2mm (2.25in)
Wheels		5.50J x 14
Tyres	185SR x 14R, tubeless	205R x 14R, tubeless
Fuel tank capacity		59 litres (13 gallons)
Electrical		
System		12 volt 45 Amp alternator
Battery		12 volt 44 amp/hour
Turning circle	11m (36ft)	12.1m (39ft)

There were four basic models of the CF van and light truck range, the CF230, CF250, CF280, and CF350, differing from the basic two models shown in the above specifications by power units, payloads and gross vehicle weights. Type 97F70 differed from the base 97170 by the installation of the 2.3 litre diesel engine and increased output 12V battery. Type 97370 differed from the base type 97170 by installation of the 2.3 litre 4 cylinder petrol engine, increase in brake size and tyre size. Type 97670 differed from the base type 97170 by installation of the 2.3 litre diesel engine, increase in brake size and tyre size. The 97770 differed from the base type 97570 by the installation of the 2.3 litre diesel engine, increase in the rear brake width and the difference in tyre size and wheels. The 97K70 differed from the base type 97570 by installation of the 2.3 litre diesel engine, increase in rear brake width and a difference in tyre size, also an increase in battery output.
Gross vehicle weights vary from 2340kg to 4860kg (10716 lb), gross train weight.

TRUCKS – 'KB' series

The 'KB' series provided a tough normal control pick-up capable of carrying every-day commercial duties with a payload of 1225kg (2701 lb) for the standard 4 x 2 model, KB26, and a payload capacity of 1140kg (2514 lb) for the diesel version, KBD26.
The two power units available were the 1.6 litre petrol, developing 79 b.h.p and the diesel of 2 litre, developing 46 b.h.p. Four speed gearbox synchromesh of all forward gears.
Ladder type chassis frame tapered at the front and kick-up at the front and rear axle locations. Brakes of the dual circuit design with independent circuits for front and rear hydraulically operated wheel brake assemblies. Servo assisted.
Passenger car type comfort with the usual electrics and equipment.
Gearbox ratios – 1st, 4.7:1; 2nd, 2.84:1; 3rd, 1.63:1; 4th, 1.0:1; reverse 4.35:1.
With a similar specification was the four wheel drive version of the pick-up, the model KB41, with a shorter wheelbase of 104.3in, against the longer wheelbase of 117.9in for the KB26.

Models	KB26	KB41	KB41 (4 x 4)	KBD41 (4 x 4)
Type	95G26	95G41	95G41	95D41
Wheelbase	2.995mm (117.9in)		2.65mm (104.3in)	
GVW	2350kg (5181 lb)			
Kerb weight	1125kg (2486 lb)	1210kg (2668 lb)		1295kg (2855lb)
Payload (approx)	1225kg (2710 lb)	1140kg (2513 lb)		1055kg (2326lb)
Engine	1.6 litre petrol		2 litre petrol	
Gearbox	4 speed column change		4 speed floor	
Rear axle ratio	4.55:1			
Front axle ratio	N/A		4.55:1	
Transfer gearbox	N/A		1:1 & 1.87: (4 x 4) & 1:1 (4 x 2)	
Front suspension	Independent wishbone arms, torsion bar springs. Stabiliser bar			
Rear suspension	Semi-elliptic leaf springs - 4 leaves			
Brakes				
System	Dual circuit. Hydraulically operated. Servo assisted			
Front diameter	208mm (8.2in) discs			
Front width	110mm (4.3in)inner; 102mm (4 in) outer			
Rear diameter	254mm (10in) drum			
Rear width	50mm (1.97in) shoe			
Wheels	5J x 14			
Tyres	185R x 14C. 8 ply			
Fuel tank capacity	70 litres (15.4g)		50 litres (11 gall)	
Electrical				
System	12V. 35A alternator		12V. 40A alt	
Battery	12V 60 amp/hour		12V 80 amp/hour	
Turning circle	11.6m (38ft.1in)		10.6m (34ft.7in)	

The 'K' series had 4 versions, two 4x2 and two 4x4, differing mainly by power unit and fuel tank capacity.
Types 95D41 and 95D26 differ by diesel engine installation and larger alternator capacity.

TRUCKS – 'TK' series

The 'TK' series was the most successful truck range for a medium weight. A variety of wheelbases and gross vehicle weights were offered. There were three power units; Bedford diesels of 3.6 litre, 5.4 litre and 8.2 litre. Four and five speed gearboxes, one Bedford and three Turner. Gearbox ratios –

Bedford	Turner T5A 3262	T5A3264	T5A 3256
4 speed	5 speed overdrive	5 speed wide ratio	5 speed wide ratio
1st 7.06:1	5.87:1	6.47:1	6.06:1
2nd 3.33:1	3.26:1	3.26:1	3.5:1
3rd 1.71:1	1.81:1	1.81:1	1.8:1
4th 1.0:1	1.0:1	1.0:1	1.0:1
5th N/A	0.85:1	0.85:1	0.8:1
Rev 7.06:1	5.98:1	6.0:1	6.0:1

Five wheelbases from 2.91m (115in) to 4.242m (167in). Flat topped ladder type frame with mild steel channel section side members and alligator jaw cross members. Cold squeeze rivetted construction. Two rear axle types – Bedford single speed spiral bevel gear drive, Bedford single speed hypoid bevel gear drive. Brakes vary from hydraulic with servo assistance and air pressure hydraulically operated.

Models	TK570	TK750	TK860	
Type	SHG1BCO	SHIL2BCO	SJM2BCO	SJM3BCO
			(code 770/804)	
Wheelbase	2.921m (115in)	3.429m (135in)	3.835m (151in)	
Kerb weight	2180kg (4807 lb)	2460kg (5424 lb)	2789kg (6150lb)	2881kg (6353lb)
GVW	5690kg (12546 lb)		7490kg (16151 lb)	
Payload (approx)	3510kg (7739 lb)	5030kg(11091lb)	4701kg(10365lb)	4609kg (10163lb)
Clutch diameter	254mm (10in)		330mm (13in)	
Engine	3.6 litre diesel		5.4 litre diesel	
Gearbox	4 speed wide ratio		5 speed overdrive	
Rear axle ratio	4.375:1	6.2:1	4.63:1	
Front suspension	Semi-elliptic leaf spring. Multi leaf			
Rear suspension	Semi-elliptic leaf spring. Multi leaf			
Brakes				
System	Hydraulic operated. Vacuum servo assisted		Air pressure	
Front diameter	330mm (13in)			
Front width	76.2mm (3in)		80.8mm (3.18in)	
Rear diameter	307.9mm (12.13in)		330mm (13in)	
Rear width	76.2mm (3in)		106.2mm (4.18in)	
Wheels	5.50F x 16		6.006 x 16	
Tyres	7.00 x 16 radial		7.50 x 16 radial	
Fuel tank	54.6 litres (12g)		118 litres (26 gall)	
Electrical				
System	12 volt. 35 amp alternator			
Battery	12 volt 95 amp/hour		12 volt 128 amp/hour	
Turning circle	11.5m (37.72ft)	13.44m (44 ft)	14.93m (49ft)	

Models	TK1000		TK1260	
Type	SJN3BCO	SJR6BCO	SJR3BCO	SLR3DCO
Wheelbase	3.835m (151in)	3.048m (120in)	4.242m (167in)	
Kerb weight	3073kg (6776 lb)	3293kg (7261lb)	3454kg (7617lb)	3745kg (8258lb)
GVW	10000kg (22050 lb)		12550kg (27673 lb)	
Payload (approx)	6927kg (15274 lb)	9257kg (20412lb)	9096kg(20057lb)	8805kg (19415lb)
Clutch diameter	330mm (13in)		356mm (14in)	
Engine	5.4 litre diesel		8.2 litre diesel	
Gearbox	5 speed overdrive			
Rear axle ratio	5.29:1	6.8:1	5.83:1	
Front suspension	Semi-elliptic leaf springs			
Rear suspension	Semi-elliptic leaf springs with helpers			
Brakes	Hydraulic	Hydraulic. Air operated. Independent circuits		
System	Air assisted			
Front diameter	358.6mm (14.12in)		409mm (16.12in)	

Front width	80.8mm (3.18in)	106.2mm (4.18in)
Rear diameter	358.6mm (14.12in)	409mm (16.12in)
Rear width	106.2mm (4.18in)	127mm (5in)
Wheels	B6.00 x 17	B6.50 x 20
Tyres	8.25 x 17 radial	9.00 x 20 radials
Fuel tank capacity	118 litre (26g)	204.57 litres (45.6 gallons)
Electrical		
System	12volt 35 amp alternator	24 v 31.8 amp
Battery	12 volt 128 amp/hour	2 x 12v 95 amp/hour
Turning circle	14.17m (46.5ft) 13.8m (45.25ft)	18.1m (59ft.5in)

Models	TK1260	
Type	SJR4BCO	SLR4DCO
Wheelbase	4.902m (193in)	
Kerb weight	3592kg (7920 lb)	3878kg (8551 lb)
GVW	12550kg (276678 lb)	
Payload (approx)	8958kg (19752 lb)	8672kg (19122 lb)
Clutch diameter	330mm (13in)	356mm (14in)
Engine	5.4 litre diesel	8.2 litre diesel
Gearbox	5 speed overdrive	
Rear axle ratio	6.8:1	5.83:1
Front suspension	Semi-elliptic leaf springs	
Rear suspension	Semi-elliptic leaf springs with helpers	
Brakes		
System	Hydraulic. Air operated	
Front diameter	409.4mm (16.12in)	
Front width	106.2mm (4.18in)	
Rear diameter	409.4mm (16.12in)	
Rear width	127mm (5in)	
Wheels	B6.50 x 20	
Tyres	9.00 x 20 - radial	
Fuel tank capacity	204.57 litres (45.6 gallons)	
Electrical		
System	12V 35A alternator	24V 31.8A alternator
Battery	12V 128 amp/hour	2 x 12V 95 amp/hour
Turning circle	20.8m (68.25ft)	

TRUCKS – 'TL' series

The 'TL' series was a medium range of vehicles continuing from the very successful 'TK' range, but offering more to the operator. Rigid type vehicles spanned from 5.6 tons to 16 tons gross vehicle weight and articulated units from 16 to 19 tons gross combination weights. All covered by 32 model variants.

Seven power units were available: three Bedford petrol engines of 3.5 litres, developing 83 b.h.p.; 3.5 litre, developing 80.5 b.h.p.; and 4.9 litre, developing 113 b.h.p: four Bedford diesel engines of 3.6 litre, developing 65 b.h.p.; 5.4 litre, developing 98 b.h.p; 8.2 litre, developing 130 b.h.p; and 8.2 litre, developing 150 b.h.p.

A wide range of gearboxes to combine with the power units to provide the appropriate performance with the most suitable drive line for the various models. Bedford four speed available both in close and wide ratios synchromesh; Turner five speed gearboxes, T5A models available with overdrive, wide ratios and close ratios; Eaton five speed 542 model with overdrive, and the model 475 available with direct drive or overdrive. To complete the drive line a series of Bedford rear axles fully floating single speed with either spiral bevel gear or hypoid bevel gear drives, and Eaton 16 series two speed axles.

Brakes for medium range models to the TL1470 at 10.5 tons gross, air operated hydraulic brakes, and the heavier model the TL1630, 16 tons and TL 1930, 19 tons, GCW, full air operated brakes.

All steel tilt cab, the first time Bedford had used a tilt type cab.

Models	TL570	TL750	TL860
Type	DDG1BGO	DDL2BGO	DJM2BGO
			(C234/770/840)
Wheelbase	2.92m (115in)	3.42m (135in)	
Kerb weight	2251kg (4963 lb)	2511kg (5537 lb)	2947kg (6498 lb)
GVW	5690kg (12546 lb)	7490kg (16515 lb)	
Payload (approx)	3439kg (7583 lb)	4979kg (10979 lb)	4543kg (10017 lb)
Engine	3.5 litre petrol	5.4 litre diesel	5.4 litre diesel
Gearbox	Bedford four speed		
Rear axle ratio	4.38:1	4.71:1	4.38:1
Front suspension	Semi-elliptic taper leaf springs		
Rear suspension	Semi-elliptic multi leaf springs		
Brakes			
System	Air operated hydraulic wheel brakes		
Front diameter	330.2mm (123in)		
Front width	76.2mm (3in)	80mm (3.18in)	
Rear diameter	330.2mm (13in)		
Rear width	76.2mm (3in)	106mm (4.18in)	
Wheels	5.50F x 16	6.00G x 16	
Tyres	7.00R x 16 radial	7.50R x 16 radial	
Fuel tank capacity	54.6 litre	118 litre	
Electrical			
System	12 volt 35A alternator		
Battery	12V 60 amp/hour	12V 128 amp/hour	
Turning circle	11.5m (38ft.4in)	13.44m (44ft)	

There were two versions of the TL570, standard, as shown, and type DMG1BGO (C561), differing by the installation of the Bedford 3.6 litre diesel engine and a larger capacity output battery.

There were four versions of the TL750, standard, as shown, and types DHL2BGO (C561), differing by the installation of the Bedford 3.6 litre diesel engine, Turner five speed gearbox and a larger capacity output battery; DLA3CGO (C234), differing by the installation of the Bedford 8.2 litre diesel engine, Turner five speed gearbox, heavier output battery and 3.84m (131in) wheelbase.

There were ten versions of the TL860, standard, as shown, and nine others, differing in engines, gearboxes, gross vehicle weights and wheelbases.

Models	TL1000	TL1020	TL1260
Type	DFN3BGO	DLW3CGO (C234)	DFR6BGO
Wheelbase		3.84m (151in)	3.05m (120in)
Kerb weight	3080kg (6791 lb)	3666kg (8083 lb)	3312kg (7303 lb)
GVW	10000kg (22050 lb)	10200kg (22491 lb)	12550kg (27673 lb)
Payload (approx)	6920kg (15258 lb)	6534kg (14407 lb)	9238kg (20369 lb)
Engine	4.9 litre petrol	8.2 litre diesel	4.9 litre petrol
Gearbox	Bedford 4 speed	Turner 5 speed	Bedford 4 speed
Rear axle ratio	5.29:1	3.89:1	6.83:1
Front suspension		Semi-elliptic. Taper leaf spring	
Rear suspension		Semi-elliptic. Multi-leaf spring	
Brakes			
System		Air operated hydraulic. Independent circuits	
Front diameter		358.6mm (14in)	409.4mm (16in)
Front width		80.8mm (3.18in)	106.2mm (4.18in)
Rear diameter		358.6mm (14in)	409.4mm (16in)
Rear width		106.2mm (4.18in)	127mm (5in)
Wheels		B6.0 x 17	B6.5 x 22.5
Tyres		8.25R x 17 radial	10R22.5 tubeless
Fuel tank capacity		118 litre (26 galls)	150 litre (33 g)
Electrical			
System	12V 35A alternator	24V 35A alternator	12V 35A alternator
Battery	12V 75 amp/hour	2x12V 95 amp/hour	12V 35 amp/hour
Turning circle		14.17m (46.5ft)	13.8m (45.25ft)

There were three versions of the TL1000, standard, as shown; type DJN3BGO (C234), differing by the installation of the Bedford 5.4 litre (105) diesel engine and a larger capacity output battery, also the Bedford 4 speed gearbox with close ratios; and type DJN3BGO (C561), differing by the installation of the Bedford 5.4 litre (1235) diesel engine, larger capacity output battery, Turner five speed gearbox. There were two versions of the TL1020, standard, as shown, and type DLW3CGO (C561), differing by the installation of the Bedford 5.4 litre (135) diesel engine, a smaller output battery.

There were nineteen versions of the TL1260, standard, as shown, and 18 others, differing in engines, gearboxes, gross vehicle weights and wheelbases.

Models	TL1500	TL1630	TL1630 Tractor	TL1930 Tractor
Type	DMT2DGO(C234)	DMVTDGO(C234)	DJP8BGO(C234)	DLR8JGO(C234)
Wheelbase	3.4m (134in)	3.76m (148in)	2.44m (96in)	
Kerb weight	4394kg (9689 lb)	4754kg (10482lb)	3124kg (6888 lb)	3469kg (7649 lb)
GVW	15000kg (33075 lb)		16260kg (35853 lb)	19310kg (42578 lb)
Payload (approx)	10606kg (23386 lb)	11506kg (25370lb)	13096kg(28877lb)	15841kg(34929 lb)*
Engine	8.2 litre (175) diesel		5.4litre diesel	8.2 litre(130)diesel
Gearbox	Turner 5 speed T5C4283		Bedford 4 spd CR	Turner 5 spdT5A
Rear axle ratio	6.17:1		6.83:1	5.57/7.75:1 2spd
Front suspension	Semi-elliptic springs. Taper leaves (2)			
Rear suspension	Semi-elliptic springs. Multi-leaf. Helpers - TL1500/TL1630			
Brakes				
System	Air operated hydraulic		Full air operated	
Front diameter	393.7mm (15.5in)		409.4mm (16in)	
Front width	127mm (5in)	177.8mm (7in)	106.2mm (4.18in)	
Rear diameter	393.7mm (15.5in)		409.4mm (16in)	
Rear width	152.4mm (6in)	203.2mm (8in)	127mm (5in)	
Wheels	7.5 x 22.5		B6.00 x 22.5	B6.5 x 22.5
Tyres	11R22.5 tubeless radial		8R22.5 tubeless	9R22.5 tubeless
Fuel tank capacity	209 litre (46 galls)		154.6 litres (34 gall)	
Electrics				
System	24V 35A alternator		12V 35A alt	24V 35A alternator
Battery	2 x 12V 95 amp/hour		12V 128 amp/hour	2x12V 95 amp/hour
Turning circle	15m (49.25ft)	14.63m (48ft)	9.36m (30.75ft)	9.75m (31ft.11in)

* Includes gear, trailer and payload

There were three versions of the TL1500, standard, as shown; type DMT3DGO(C234); and type DMT4DGO(C234), both differing by the wheelbase.

There are five versions of the TL1630, standard, as shown, and types DMV7DGO(C234); DMV1DGO(C234); DMV2DGO(C234); and DMV3DGO(C234), all differing by the wheelbase.

There were two versions of the TL1630 tractor, standard, as shown, and type DJP8BGO(C561), differing by the installation of a Bedford 5.4 litre (135) diesel engine.

There were two versions of the TL1930, standard, as shown, and type DLR8JGO(C561), differing by the installation of the Bedford 5.4 litre (135) diesel engine and increased output battery.

TRUCKS - 'TM' series

The 'TM' range embodied a whole series of important engineering features. Inside the tilt cab higher standards of comfort and convenience were designed into the range. Regular cab version, narrow in width, full width version and a full width sleeper cab.

The 'TM' range, with a choice of gross weights, whether vehicle, combination or train, power units, matched with appropriate drive lines (gearbox and rear axles), made it one of the most comprehensive heavy truck ranges offered to the operator. There were four wheelers (4x2), single or double drive six wheelers (6x2 or 6x4), rated for gross vehicle weights from 15 to 26 tonne, gross train weights up to 44 tonne and tractor units available for combination weights from 20 to 44 tonne.

Power units offered were the Bedford's own diesel turbocharged diesels, two versions; Detroit Diesels 6V-71, two versions of the model 6V-92, the TTA and the TA; and Cummins E255, E290 and E370, all turbocharged units. Drive lines skilfully matched with the power units were Eaton six speed, Turner six speed, Fuller nine and thirteen speed gearboxes and Bedford's own rear axle, two versions; Eaton 18300 series and the 20/22; and Rockwell U180 rear axles.

The correct combinations of power drive lines gave each model the performance required to the gross weights and class of operation.

Models	TM1700	TM1900	TM2600 (6x2)	TM2600 (6x4)
Type	EMV3D0(C234)	ESX3TFD0	HMX3VD0(C234)	
Wheelbase	5.23m (206in)		5.08m (200in)	4.45m (175in)
Kerb weight	5195kg (11446 lb)	6379kg (14067 lb)	6332kg (13955 lb)	6535kg (14403 lb)
GVW	16260kg (35840 lb)		24390kg (53780 lb)	
Payload (approx)	11065kg (2493 lb)	9881kg (21772 lb)	18058kg (398041b)	17855kg(39357 lb)
Engine	8.2 litre diesel	6V-92TTA Detroit	Bedford 8.2 litre diesel	
Gearbox	Turner 6 speed	Fuller 9 speed	Eaton 6 speed	
Rear axle ratio	6.83:1	3.07:1	7.2:1	7.17:1
Front suspension	Minimum leaf. Semi-elliptic leaf springs			
Rear suspension	Semi-elliptic leaf springs			
Brakes				
System	Full air operated brake system			
Front diameter	394mm (15.5in)		394mm (15.5in)	
Front width	177.8mm (7in)	200mm (7.87in)	177.8mm (7in)	
Rear diameter	394mm (15.5in)		394mm (15.5in)	
Rear width	203mm (8in)	200mm (7.87in)	203.8mm (8in)	203.2mm (8in)
Wheels	7.5x22.5	B8.5x20	7.5x22.5	
Tyres	11R22.5tubelessR	12.00x20 Radial	11Rx22.5tubeless radial	
Fuel tank capacity	139 litre (30.5g)	266 litre (58.5g)	195.5 litre (43g)	
Electrics				
System	24V 35A alt	24V 31.8A alt	24V 35A alternator	
Battery	2x12V 95amp/hr	2x12V 125 amp/hr	2x12V 95 amp/hr	
Turning circle	19.5m (64ft)	21.3m (69ft10in)	19.5m (64ft)	

'TM' series had 30 versions differing generally by power units, gearboxes, rear axle ratios, wheelbases. However, braking systems differ only in front & rear brake shoe width, but in the case of articulated tractor units, the braking system may vary according to the legislation.

TM1700 had 6 versions: standard, as shown, and other types differing by engines, gearboxes, suspensions and wheelbase.

TM1900 had two versions: standard, as shown, and one differing by gross vehicle weight and payload.

TM2600 sixwheeler 6x2 and 6x4 had 6 versions: standard, as shown, and five other types differing by engines, gearboxes, suspension, tyres and electrical equipment.

Models	TM2500	TM3250	TM3650	TM440
Type	EMV8VDO(C234)	ENV8TDO	EWV8MFO	ESX8TFO
Wheelbase	3.0m (118in)		3.12m (123in)	
Kerb weight	4892kg (10797lb)	5191kg (11446lb)	5798kg (12790lb)	6350kg (14000lb)
GCW	25000kg (55104lb)	32520kg (71680lb)	36500kg (80483lb)	44000kg (97020 lb)
Payload (approx)			-	
Engine	Bedford 8.2 litre diesel		Detroit 6V-71 d	Detroit 6V-92TTA
Gearbox	Eaton 6 speed		Fuller nine speed	
Rear axle ratio	7.2:1	4.87:1	5.43:1	3.7:1
Front suspension	Minimum leaf. Semi-elliptic springs			
Rear suspension	Semi-elliptic leaf springs			
Brakes				
System	Full air operated brake system			
Front diameter	394mm (15.5in)			
Front width	203.2mm (8in)			
Rear diameter	394mm (15in)			
Rear width	203.2mm (8in)			
Wheels	7.5x22.5		B8.5 x 22.5	
Tyres	11Rx22.5 tubeless radial		12.00 x 20 radial	
Fuel tank capacity	195 litres (43 g)		340 litres (75g)	322 litres (73g)
Electrics				
System	24V 35A alternator		24V 31.8A alternator	
Battery	2x12V 95 amp/hr		2x12V 125 amp/h	
Turning circle	12.5m (41ft)			

TM2500 and 3250 had one standard version, as shown

TM3650 had 4 versions: standard, as shown, and three other types differing by engines, gearboxes, wheelbases and fuel tank capacities.

TM4400 had 4 versions: standard, as shown, and three others differing by engines and electrical equipment.

BUSES – 'V', 'S' and 'Y' series

Bedford buses were always a favourite with the small operators. Initially based on the commercial goods vehicle models, eventually developing into specially designed chassis for bus and coach operation.

'V' series with wheelbases of 4.166m (164in) and 4.902m (193in); forward mounted power units; gross vehicle weights from 6590kg (14537 lb) to 10920kg (24080 lb), model versions VAS and VAM.

'S' series: SB with one wheelbase of 5.486 (216in); forward mounted power units; based on the components used on the 'S' series goods vehicles; gross vehicle weights of 9090kg (20048 lb) and 9960kg (21952 lb).

'Y' series with wheelbases 4.902m (193in) and 5.639m (222in). Underfloor midship mounted power units. Gross vehicle weights from 10180kg (22444 lb) to 12500kg (27552 lb).

Models	VAS	VAM	SB
Type	PJK1BZO	BLP2DZO	NJM2BZO
Wheelbase	4.166m (164in)	4.902m (193in)	5.486m (216in)
Kerb weight	2487kg (5484 lb)	3534kg (7792 lb)	2930kg (6461 lb)
GVW	6590kg (14531 lb)	10180kg (22447 lb)	9090kg (20043 lb)
Payload (approx)		-	
Engine	5.4 litre (100)D	8.2 litre (140)D	5.4 litre (100)D
Gearbox	Bedford 4 spCR	Bedford 5 sp	Bedford 4 sp WR
Rear axle ratio	4.63:1	5.28:1	5.83:1
Front suspension		Semi-elliptic leaf springs	
Rear suspension		Semi-elliptic leaf springs	
Brakes			
System	Air hydraulic	Full air operated	Air hydraulic
Front diameter	332mm (13.1in)	394mm (15.5in)	409mm (16in)
Front width	81mm (3.19in)	152mm (5.98in)	106mm (4.18in)
Rear diameter	332mm (13.1in)	394mm (15.5in)	409mm (16in)
Rear width	106mm (4.18in)	152mm (5.98in)	127mm (5in)
Wheels	6.00G x 16	B6.50 x 20	B6.0 x 20
Tyres	7.50 x 16 radial	9.00 x 20 radial	8.25 x 20 radial
Fuel tank capacity	118 litres (26g)	209 litres (46g)	118 litres (26g)
Electrics			
System	12V 100A alt	24V 35A alt	12V 100A alt
Battery	2-12V 195 amp/hr	4-12V 135 amp/hr	2-12V 195 amp/hr
Turning circle	15.5m (50ft10in)	18m (59ft1in)	19.6m (64ft4in)

Both 'VAS' and 'S' SB had two versions, standard, and one differing by engine, gearbox and electrical equipment.
'VAM' had one version only.

139

Models	YMP	YMT	YNT
Type	YMP2DZO	YMT3DZO	YNT3VZO
Wheelbase	4.902m (193in)	5.639m (222in)	
Kerb weight	3771kg (8315 lb)	4243kg (9356 lb)	4274kg (9424 lb)
GVW	10180kg (22447 lb)	12500kg (27563 lb)	
Payload (approx)		-	
Engine	8.2 litre (160 diesel)		8.2 litre (205)D
Gearbox	5 speed overdrive		6 speed overdrive
Rear axle ratio	5.83:1		5.28:1
Front suspension	Semi-elliptic leaf springs		
Rear suspension	Semi-elliptic leaf springs		
Brakes			
System	Full air operated. Independent circuits		
Front diameter	394mm (15.5in)		
Front width	152mm (6in)	178mm (7in)	
Rear diameter	394mm (15.5in)		
Rear width	152mm (6in)	203mm (8 in)	
Wheels	B6.50 x 20	B7.00 x 20	
Tyres	9.00 x 20 radial	10.00 x 20 radial	
Fuel tank capacity	209 litres (46g)	255 litres (56g)	
Electrics			
System	24V 58A alternator		
Battery	4 - 12V 135/amp/hour		
Turning circle	18m (59ft1in)	17.5m (57ft5in)	

There was only one version of the 'Y' series for each model